The Anthropology of Language

Chpt. 2 + ?'s

WORKBOOK/READER

HARRIET JOSEPH OTTENHEIMER

KANSAS STATE UNIVERSITY

THOMSON

WADSWORTH

Australia • Canada • Mexico • Singapore • Spain • United Kingdom • United States

THOMSON
―――――✦―――――™
WADSWORTH

The Anthropology of Language
An Introduction to Linguistic Anthropology
Workbook and Reader
Harriet Joseph Ottenheimer
Kansas State University

Publisher: Eve Howard
Senior Acquisitions Editor: Lin Marshall
Assistant Editor: Nicole Root
Editorial Assistant: Kelly McMahon
Technology Project Manager: Dee Dee Zobian
Advertising Project Manager: Linda Yip
Project Manager, Editorial Production: Katy German
Art Director: Maria Epes

Print Buyer: Lisa Claudeanos
Permissions Editor: Chelsea Junget
Production Service: G & S Book Services
Text Designer: Diane Beasley
Copy Editor: G & S Book Services
Cover Designer: Laurie Anderson
Printer: West Group

Printed in The United States of America
4   5   6   7   09   08   07   06

For more information about our products,
contact us at:
Thomson Learning Academic Resource Center
1-800-423-0563

For permission to use material from this text or product,
submit a request online at
http://www.thomsonrights.com.
Any additional questions about permissions can be
submitted by email to **thomsonrights@thomson.com.**

ISBN-13: 978-0-534-59437-4
ISBN-10: 0-534-59437-9

Thomson Higher Education
10 Davis Drive
Belmont, CA 94002-3098
USA

Asia (including India)
Thomson Learning
5 Shenton Way
#01-01 UIC Building
Singapore 068808

Australia/New Zealand
Thomson Learning Australia
102 Dodds Street
Southbank, Victoria 3006
Australia

Canada
Thomson Nelson
1120 Birchmount Road
Toronto, Ontario M1K 5G4
Canada

UK/Europe/Middle East/Africa
Thomson Learning
High Holborn House
50–51 Bedford Row
London WC1R 4LR
United Kingdom

Latin America
Thomson Learning
Seneca, 53
Colonia Polanco
11560 Mexico
D.F. Mexico

Spain (including Portugal)
Thomson Paraninfo
Calle Magallanes, 25
28015 Madrid, Spain

For Raia

CONTENTS

Chapter 1

LINGUISTIC ANTHROPOLOGY   1

Chapter 2

LANGUAGE AND CULTURE   15

Chapter 3

SOUNDS   29

Chapter 4

WORDS AND SENTENCES

50

Chapter 5

LANGUAGE IN ACTION 70

Chapter 6

NONVERBAL COMMUNICATION 79

Chapter 10

DOING LINGUISTIC ANTHROPOLOGY 130

PREFACE

INTRODUCTION TO THE MATERIALS

The Anthropology of Language is a unique package consisting of a textbook, a workbook/reader, and a companion website designed to make the intersection of linguistics and anthropology accessible and interesting to undergraduate students. It is an entry-level introduction to the field of linguistic anthropology that should appeal to students from a wide variety of fields and at a wide variety of levels, from freshmen to seniors. The package is based on my thirty-plus years of experience teaching an introductory course in linguistic anthropology at Kansas State University. The textbook is designed to introduce basic concepts as succinctly as possible. The workbook/reader and the different guided projects described in it challenge students to think critically about basic concepts and guide them to practical ways of applying their new knowledge to everyday situations. Projects and exercises are doable, enjoyable, and sufficiently challenging to keep student interest high. The idea is to get students to actively apply the concepts to their everyday lives as effectively and as early as possible. The companion website provides links to additional articles and sites of interest, as well as to study guides and review questions for students. The entire package provides a comprehensive, user-friendly introduction to linguistic anthropology for undergraduates.

ORGANIZATION OF THE PACKAGE

All of the components of the package (workbook/reader, textbook, and companion website) are carefully linked together. The workbook/reader elaborates on points made in the textbook; and the textbook points students to the workbook/reader for ways to practice the skills they are learning, for readings that provide deeper understanding of issues raised in each chapter, and for directions for semester-long guided projects that give students ways to test their skills in real life or special group situations. Both the textbook and the workbook/reader point to the companion website, where students will find additional exercises and readings, links to other relevant websites, study questions, hints for how to complete various sections of the guided projects, and key words to guide them in searching through the readings in the InfoTrac® collection of articles.

THE WORKBOOK/READER

The workbook/reader provides classic and contemporary exercises and readings as well as information on how to complete the semester-long guided projects. Because each reading, exercise, or guided project module has been carefully chosen to illuminate or expand on the basic concepts introduced in the textbook, it is important for students to consult their textbooks for hints about the readings, exercises, and projects. Exercises range from beginning to intermediate in skill level, with only a few advanced exercises included. The aim is to keep students interested by presenting them with simple, solvable puzzles rather than to overwhelm them with the complexities of language. Highly motivated students will appreciate the challenge of the advanced exercises. Most students will want to stop before completing the KiSwahili syntax exercise, for example, but a few will relish the challenge of forging ahead with it.

The Readings

Each reading is carefully selected to coordinate with a chapter in the textbook. A brief introduction to each reading highlights key points to look for and helps to connect the reading with important points from the textbook. Readings may expand further on issues introduced in the textbook or may provide examples of how those issues or techniques apply in actual or even in make-believe situations. For a thorough understanding of the issues, it is important for students to refer to the textbook chapter in question and be sure they understand the relationship between it and the reading. For example, where the workbook/reader provides a reading on English Only laws passed in 1921 in Nebraska, the textbook provides an in-depth discussion of linguistic chauvinism in the United States, setting it into wider historical and contemporary contexts, including a discussion of linguistic identity and the ways that individuals and groups confront such issues as well as the ways that individuals and groups may choose to assert their ethnic, national, or other identities through language use. Where the textbook provides a basic introduction to phonetics and phonology, the workbook/reader provides additional material that will take students further in their understanding of phonetic charts, phonetic characters, phonemes, and allophones.

The Exercises

Each reading is followed by a set of exercises. Discussion/writing questions encourage students to think about the reading or about key issues in the chapter and to formulate responses to share with their classmates or to hand in for grading. Exercises following the English Only article, for example, encourage students to think and write about ways in which restrictive language laws may have affected their own families, and about whether forcing people to give up their language has led to increased national unity. Exercises following the Conklin article encourage students to explore linguistic relativity and linguistic determinism on their own and with the help of their conversation partners or friends.

The more traditional linguistic exercises are also keyed to specific sections of the textbook. For example, the exercises for working with phonetic charts enhance students' understanding of the discussion of phonetics in the textbook, while the exercise for reconstructing protolanguages is an enjoyable way for students to test their understanding of the textbook's presentation of this methodology, as well as to gain insight into how linguistic anthropologists use historical material.

Most of the workbook exercises are generally simple and easy to complete. One good way to use them is to ask students to try the first one in a series (for example, the first of the phonetic exercises) on their own. You can then review that exercise in class and then continue by solving several more at the beginning of a class period. You can stop short of solving the last one in a series and let the students complete it on their own and hand it in for grading. One series of workbook exercises is drawn from a single language (KiSwahili). Many students find that they enjoy the way this particular group of exercises reveals the interconnectedness of different levels of analysis. Many also appreciate the opportunity to delve just a little more deeply into one language.

The Web Exercises

Web exercises in each chapter point students to the companion website for additional links that they can follow and additional projects that they can do. For example, in the chapter on fieldwork, students are advised to follow links on the companion website to read about the field experiences of cultural and linguistic anthropologists and to write about, or discuss with their classmates, some of the challenges that anthropologists face in getting started in fieldwork or in adjusting frames of reference. Such web-based exercises connect closely with the discussion in the textbook on fieldwork and ethnocentricity, as well as with the reading in the workbook on fieldwork and communication. Web-based exercises for this chapter also encourage students to explore the American Anthropological Association's statement on ethics and to review this statement in conjunction with the textbook's discussion of ethics in fieldwork. Each chapter contains similar exercises designed to encourage students to use the web to expand their knowledge and understanding.

Web exercises also encourage students to search the Wadsworth InfoTrac database for articles relevant to the issues discussed in each chapter. The Chapter 1 exercises, for example, suggest that students explore the InfoTrac database for articles about fieldwork and about Franz Boas and the beginnings of linguistic anthropology in the United States. Creative students and instructors will be able to think of other ideas for article searches. Articles on ethics, for example, might also be suggested for Chapter 1. Students should be encouraged to follow their leads and to explore as widely and deeply as their own interests take them.

The Guided Projects: Language Creating and Conversation Partnering

Each workbook/reader chapter concludes with instructions for how to complete the relevant module(s) in two semesterlong guided projects. I have designed these guided projects to help students apply the skills they are learning to specific situations. I find that such application really helps students to retain their new knowledge and to understand its importance. Each of the guided projects has a set of specific assignments (or modules) that the students complete as they work through the relevant chapters. Additional guidelines and suggestions for using these projects and their modules will be housed (and updated) in the instructor's resource section of the companion website. Students find these to be engaging and fun, perhaps even more so than reading the text or doing the workbook exercises! You can assign one or both of these projects, depending on your resources and time limitations. I generally try to do both projects in one semester, but it takes careful coordination. Having a teaching assistant, for example, is invaluable for help in keeping track of which groups are doing what, or how conversation partners are getting along. You should also note that it is not necessary to use absolutely every module in a guided project, especially in the conversation partnering project. Students comment favorably on how much these two projects have helped them to grasp the basic concepts and understand the applications of linguistic anthropology to everyday life. The guided projects include the following.

The Language Creating Project
The language creating project guides students in the process of creating a "real" language in a group setting. There are ten units in this collection (sound charts, allophones, words and affixes, sentence construction, transformations, dialectical differences, greetings/taboos/euphemisms, social differences in languages, gestures and teasing, borrowing, and orthography). It is best to use as many of these as possible during the course of the semester; I use them all. At the end of the semester I have each group present a short skit using their invented language, and I ask them to briefly discuss their language for the rest of the class. They are also required to turn in a project book containing all of the details of their language. These are graded primarily for internal consistency. A general in-class debriefing and discussion of language similarities and differences rounds out the experience. A question on the final exam asking students to sum up some easily remembered item from their language makes it possible to check on individual performance if necessary. Students think that this project is "really cool" or "lots of fun" and often comment on how the experience helps them to understand how languages work. One of the key benefits of the experience is the way in which it helps students to understand how phonemes and allophones work!

The Conversation Partnering Project

The conversation partnering project pairs English-speaking students in the class with international students on their campus. I ask students in my classes whose first language is not English to pair up with English-speaking students in the class. The point is to have each student paired up with someone whose first language is different from his or her own. There are currently six exercises in the collection—comparative phonology, language and culture, nonverbal communication, cross-cultural communication, language families, and dialects. Each is designed to get students talking with their conversation partners about how their languages are similar and how they are different.

I generally select three or four exercises to assign in a given semester. I find that if the language and culture exercise is done early, it helps to break the ice between the students and their conversation partners. I always include the comparative phonology exercise, asking students to draw up phonetic charts showing their own and their conversation partners' consonant inventories, because it helps them to learn a little bit about how phonetic charts really work. This leaves room for one or two other exercises, depending on the time available and what you want to stress. Here are some recent comments from students: "It was hard at first to start talking, but once we started it was hard to stop. The entire subject of the CP is really interesting." "The conversation partner is a great idea! The CP assignments were good because they made you think about and apply knowledge." I often find that students keep in touch with their conversation partners long after the class has ended.

✳ THE COMPANION WEBSITE

The companion website designed for this package provides guidelines for the projects and exercises, study questions for the readings, and links to other useful and interesting websites. It also features a pointer to InfoTrac, a database of journals where students can find additional articles of interest and relevance along with suggested key words to help them search the InfoTrac collection. Students may explore the website on their own, or instructors can assign specific readings or project segments from the website as they fit into the general flow of the course.

A separate instructor's resource area on the website (password-protected) provides additional advice and suggestions for using the exercises, readings, and guided projects. There are sample syllabi, solutions to workbook exercises, suggestions for good audiovisual materials to use in class, and specific guidelines for implementing the applied projects and for integrating them into the syllabus.

Taken together, the textbook, workbook/reader, and companion website are designed to provide an engaging, enjoyable introduction to linguistic anthropology, to encourage students to explore further on their own, and to try their hand at applying what they have learned to their everyday lives.

✳ INTEGRATION OF THE WORKBOOK/READER WITH THE TEXTBOOK

The workbook/reader should be used in conjunction with the textbook. The textbook creates the groundwork for all other elements of the package, containing introductions to the key issues, background information for understanding the contexts in which those issues are important, summaries of key points, and guidelines for completing exercises. For example, the textbook provides a basic introduction to phonetics and phonology, including some background for understanding these concepts and a discussion of their impact on anthropology in general, while the workbook provides more in-depth discussions of these analytic techniques as well as exercises that challenge students to test their developing expertise in analyzing linguistic material.

In a similar manner, the textbook provides the basics of morphological and syntactic analysis, with examples of how to complete analyses on a limited scale, while the workbook/reader provides additional real-language examples, including a series of increasingly complex exercises utilizing a single language, KiSwahili, so that students can see how complexly intertwined the various levels of analysis can be. Students who are paying close attention will notice that the Shinzwani examples in the textbook are similar to the KiSwahili examples in the workbook and will find that understanding how the Shinzwani examples work gives them a generous clue to solving the KiSwahili problems in the workbook/reader. Or instructors may prefer to point this out to students. Each chapter's exercises are foreshadowed in this way by examples and discussions in the textbook, including the exercise in decoding writing systems and the exercise in reconstructing protolanguages. Where the textbook points to the workbook/reader, the workbook/reader follows through with additional readings and exercises to expand the students' skills and understanding. In turn, the workbook/reader assumes that the students are reading the textbook and using it for guidance on how to complete the exercises and how to understand the readings.

ACKNOWLEDGMENTS

Many people have contributed to the development of this workbook/reader both directly and indirectly. I owe a debt, first of all, to those creative people under whom I studied language, literature, and linguistic anthropology: Ben Bellit, Kenneth Burke, and Stanley Edgar Hyman at Bennington College, and Marshall Durbin, Mridula Adenwala Durbin, and John Fischer at Tulane University. They have all influenced my thinking, my writing, and my choice of relevant readings, exercises, and projects in important and indescribable ways. I think they have also influenced my sense of academic playfulness in inestimable ways.

I also owe much to my students at Kansas State University, who have put up with my experiments and provided feedback over the years on the various exercises, readings, and guided projects. My early experiments with the language-creating project, in particular, were a special challenge to the students who suffered through them with me but who claimed to have enjoyed the experience nonetheless and who still tell me it was one of their most memorable academic experiences. They gave me the courage to continue experimenting and to develop a workable and enjoyable set of modules. Thanks also go to the students who contributed words in Korean, Samoan, Japanese, and other languages to improve the various workbook exercises over the years. Other students brought interesting readings to my attention or complained when a particular reading was too advanced for them or didn't expand on the textbook well enough. Particularly helpful through all these steps were Laura Bathurst, Lynda Colston, Janet Jackson, Matt Moore, Judith Pine, and Leo Walsh. I owe a special debt to my teaching assistants over the years. Each of these young people has contributed something important to the gradual development of both the textbook and the workbook/reader, including Leo Walsh, Kathiellen Gilligan, Ilija Hardage, Loubnat Affane, Anne Halvorsen, Lucas Bessire, Janet Jackson, Lynda Colston, and Nick Endicott. In addition, my department head, Len Bloomquist, and my anthropology colleagues at Kansas State University have provided support and encouragement over the years, acknowledging the importance of developing a curriculum in linguistic anthropology and maintaining a strong four-field approach to the teaching of undergraduate anthropology. They include Laura Bathurst, Janet Benson, Michael Finnegan, Bunny McBride, Pat O'Brien, Martin Ottenheimer, Harald Prins, Lauren Ritterbush, Robert Taylor, and Michael Wesch, while Debbie Hedrick has provided invaluable office assistance throughout.

Although some of the individuals who contributed ideas and materials wish to remain nameless, many others can be publicly thanked, including Loubnat Affane, Nounou Affane, Soifaoui Affane, Jun Akiyama, Barbara Babcock, Laura Bathurst, Ritu Bhatnagar, Renuka Bhatnagar, Laada Bilaniuk, Bill Bright, Jill Brody, Margie Buckner, Martin Cohen, Anis Djohar, Lelah Dushkin, Begona Echeverria, James Flanagan, Kerim Friedman, David Givens, Dinha Gorges, Nick Hale, Ilija Hardage, Wendi Haugh, Jane Hill, Barbara Hoffman, Pamela Innes, Alexandra Jaffe, Alan Joseph, Ron Kephart, Bernard Kripkee, Roger Lass, Linda Light, Lucie Lukešová, Rob MacLaury, Mike Maxwell, Bunny McBride, Emily McEwan-Fujita, Leila Monaghan, Afan Ottenheimer, Davi Ottenheimer, Martin Ottenheimer, Carsten Otto, Isaku Oweda, Bill Palmer, Jeremy Peak, Judy Pine, Harald Prins, Jana Rybková, Jan (Honza) Šabach, Jaroslav Skupnik, Ann Stirland, Jess Tauber, František Vrhel, and Brian Wygal. Many of these individuals were gracious enough to put up with my endless questions and to correct my endless mistakes as I tried to learn their languages. I will always be grateful to them for their patience and assistance. Additionally Stormy Kennedy and Kevin Snell are to be thanked for their ongoing support and assistance, especially with the workbook/reader.

Thanks are also due to those reviewers who made suggestions for strengthening the textbook: Laura Bathurst, University of California, Berkeley; Jill Brody, Louisiana State University; Martin Cohen, California State University–Northridge and Los Angeles City College; Barbara Dilly, Creighton University; James Flanagan, University of Southern Mississippi; Laura Greathouse, California State University–Fullerton; Joan Gross, Oregon State University; James Hamill, Miami University; Andy Hofling, Southern Illinois University–Carbondale; Pamela Innes, University of Wyoming; Shepherd Jenks, Albuquerque TVI Community College; Martha Macri, University of California–Davis; Nancy McKee, Washington State University; Judy Pine, Shoreline Community College and University of Washington; Cindi Sturtz Sreetharan, California State University–Sacramento; John Stolle-McAllister, University of Maryland; Isabel Terry, North Carolina State University; and Hervé Varenne, Columbia University. I appreciate the time they took to provide comments, suggestions, and, in some cases, additional examples for inclusion in the textbook.

Anita de Laguna Haviland deserves special mention, for encouraging me to think of developing a textbook/workbook combination, as does Lin Marshall, editor at Thomson/Wadsworth, for cajoling me into taking on such a project. It is in large part thanks to her careful critiques and her principled challenges that the combination has developed into its current form. I will always cherish the friendship that developed between us in the process. Thanks also to Eve Howard, publisher, as well as to Analie Barnett, Kelly McMahon, Nicole Root, and Amanda Santana, assistant editors; Sarah Harkrader and Kiely Sisk, permissions editors, Maria Epes, art director; and Katy German, production manager; and to the production team at Wadsworth. Kudos to Leah McAleer, production coordinator at G & S Book Services and her able team, including Carolyn Brown, project editor, and Julie Nemer, copyeditor, for their supremely competent attention to detail.

The greatest debt, of course, is to my family—my parents Belle and William Joseph; my husband and colleague Martin; my children Afan, Davi, and Loubnat; and my daughter-in-law Ritu, all of whom put up with my whining and complaining when fonts went wrong in the exercises or permissions were difficult to track down. Their patience was, and continues to be, enduring and gracious. It is impossible to thank them enough. Special thanks go to my granddaughter, Raia, who continues to provide wonderful examples of language learning and linguistic analysis for me to ponder.

ABOUT THE AUTHOR

Harriet Joseph Ottenheimer, professor of anthropology at Kansas State University, received a B.A. from Bennington College and a Ph.D. from Tulane University. Her research interests include music, language, and other creative and performative expressions, particularly in African American and African cultures. In addition to extended periods of field research in New Orleans and in the Comoro Islands, she has traveled and lectured widely throughout many other parts of the world. She has special interests in blues, autobiography, transcription, dictionary construction, fieldwork ethics, and ethnicity. Among her publications are *Cousin Joe: Blues from New Orleans* (with Pleasant "Cousin Joe" Joseph), a blues singer's autobiography; *The Historical Dictionary of the Comoro Islands* (with Martin Ottenheimer), an encyclopedia; "Music of the Comoro Islands: Domoni" (also with Martin Ottenheimer), in vinyl, cassette, and CD formats; *The Quorum* (with Maurice M. Martinez), a documentary film; and the *Shinzwani-English/English-Shinzwani Dictionary*, a bilingual, bidirectional dictionary data set. She has taught at the University of New Orleans, Charles University in Prague (on a visiting Fulbright appointment), and Kansas State University. At Kansas State University, she was the founding director of the interdisciplinary American Ethnic Studies Program, teaching introductory and advanced courses in that program as well as in cultural and linguistic anthropology. She has received the Kansas State University President's Award for Distinguished Service to Minority Education and the Charles Irby Award for Distinguished Service to the National Association for Ethnic Studies. She has served as president of the National Association for Ethnic Studies and the Central States Anthropological Association. She can get by (sometimes just barely) in five languages—English, Spanish, French, Russian, and Shinzwani—and she is currently attempting to learn to speak and read Czech.

STUDENT PREFACE

Dear Students: This workbook/reader is a unique combination of readings, exercises, and projects that provide an interesting and entertaining addition to the textbook, *The Anthropology of Language.* The readings have been selected for their "readability" as well as for their ability to add to your understanding of how language works and how people use it. The exercises have been selected for their "doability" and are all derived from "real" language data, providing a broad range of insight into language structure. The web exercises will take you to the companion website for this workbook/reader, where you will find additional readings, exercises, and projects as well as fascinating and timely weblinks; all sorts of additional windows will open for you on the companion website. Finally, the guided projects introduce two engaging ways to apply your developing skills and understandings to real (and imagined) situations. In one, you will learn to work with a conversation partner whose language is different from yours. In the other, you will learn how to use your understanding of linguistic structure and usage to invent and play with a fictional language.

It is very important that you use this workbook/reader together with the associated *Anthropology of Language* textbook. The textbook provides all of the basic material you will need for solving the puzzles and understanding the readings. It provides key terms and their definitions, full discussions of the issues that the readings address, and important clues for how to solve specific puzzles in the workbook/reader. The article in the workbook/reader on spelling Shinzwani, for example, gives you deeper insight into the issues involved in developing writing systems, which is discussed in the textbook. The article in the workbook/reader on cowboy proxemics adds color and life to the discussion in the textbook of how we use the space around us in everyday life. The article in the workbook/reader on Mock Spanish explores the question of hidden racism in language that is raised in the textbook in even greater depth and detail than the textbook examples, while the textbook explains the essential concept of "indexicality" so that you can follow the article and understand the subtlety of its arguments. All of the readings are closely connected with the textbook chapters, so if something is not clear in one of the readings, then you should take time to reread the associated chapter in the textbook.

As with the readings, the exercises in the workbook/reader are coordinated with the chapters in the textbook. The Shinzwani analysis in the textbook, for example, provides important clues for working with the KiSwahili puzzles in the workbook/reader. The exercise in reconstruction begins in the textbook, where the method is explained in detail and examples are given, and concludes in the workbook/reader, where the rest of the data is provided. The textbook explains the connections between language and culture and introduces several methods for analyzing these connections, while the workbook/reader provides some ways in which you can explore these connections with real data. The textbook introduces the basics of sound systems, while the workbook/reader goes into additional depth and gives you some real language data to work with. Everywhere you look, in every chapter, you will find interconnections between the workbook/reader and the textbook. Whenever you are puzzled by something in the workbook/reader, you will find clues, and sometimes even detailed answers, in the textbook. Whenever you are intrigued by something in the textbook, you should look for additional examples and exercises to try in the workbook/reader.

One set of exercises—the KiSwahili group—is designed to provide depth as well as breadth to your introduction to language analysis. If you complete all of these exercises, you will have a much better sense of how the different levels of analysis are connected throughout a single language. This is generally the case in any language you might want to study, and so knowing something of the ways that analyses at one level—for example, the level of sentences—can be affected by analyses at a different level—for example, the level of sounds, is important. Even though each level can be analyzed independently, it is important to know that all of them really do interlock. This kind of knowledge will help you significantly in any attempt you make to learn another language using the techniques and skills you have learned from linguistic anthropology.

Your instructor will be your guide through this workbook/reader, indicating which exercises and readings you should do. Feel free, of course, to do them all! Above all, have fun.

CHAPTER 1

Linguistic Anthropology

Note: Your instructor will indicate which readings, exercises, and/or projects you should do.

❊ READING

1.0 "A Goy in the Ghetto: Gentile-Jewish Communication in Fieldwork Research" by William E. Mitchell

William Mitchell's "A Goy in the Ghetto: Gentile-Jewish Communication in Fieldwork Research" is a charming introduction to the challenges of fieldwork. It also gives you an excellent sense of the importance of communicative style in different cultures and different fieldwork situations. Finally, it is an outstanding introduction to the ethical issues involved in fieldwork, with its discussion of the initial reactions that Mitchell encountered when he began inquiring into Jewish genealogy.

Early in my career as an anthropologist I joined a small team of social scientists planning a study of New York City Jewish families. An important part of my work was to interview family members in their homes. As a Gentile from Kansas I knew that my cultural background was very different from theirs, so I asked two Jewish male social scientist friends born and raised in New York City for advice. With devastating frankness I was told that my "cool Wasp manner" would "scare the wits" out of my interviewees. As Kansas men are generally open and friendly—we smile a lot—I was discomforted by their view of me. But that was only the beginning.

My body language, they said, was too detached, too placid. They were concerned that I rarely gestured and, when I did, the gesture was so small and anemic that it was barely discernible. Besides, my gestures were all wrong; they were woodenly symmetrical rather than creatively baroque. My friends insisted that if I were to work successfully with New York City Jewish families of Eastern European background, I must look more "bright-eyed" and act "more lively." And, while they assured me that my speech pattern was not as slow and heavily accented as some midwesterners', it was obvious that I must "speed it up."

If I could not make these important behavioral accommodations, the research, according to my friends, would be a disaster. The families would find me "strange" and feel "uncomfortable" and "anxious" as long as I was around. In other words, if I wanted good rapport I would have to change. "Sure you're a Gentile," they seemed to be saying. "But you don't have to act like one!"

The personal experiences on which this chapter is based took place in two separate but related studies (Leichter and Mitchell 1978; Mitchell 1980) of New York City Jewish families of Eastern European background. The parent research project, "Studies in Social Interaction," was carried out with a large group of families who were clients of the Jewish Family Service of New York. Our primary research interest was in the extent and nature of the relationships these households of parents and children had with their other relatives

Source: "A Goy in the Ghetto: Gentile-Jewish Communication in Fieldwork Research," by William E. Mitchell, in *Between Two Worlds: Ethnographic Essays on American Jewry,* ed. Jack Kugelmass, pp. 225–239. Ithaca and London: Cornell University Press. Reprinted with permission of the author.

and in the ways social workers assigned to the families intervened to support or change the relationships.

During this research we "discovered" an unusual kind of urban descent group organized as clubs called "family circles" or "cousins' clubs," and I did a separate study (Mitchell 1980) of the history, organization, and functioning of these groups that included individuals and families completely unrelated to the parent project. In both studies, I made interview visits to my informants' homes or places of business and also attended some of the family clubs' meetings and parties.[1]

How one "acts" in the research role, as my two friends knew, is a significant factor affecting rapport in behavioral research that may directly influence the outcome of the research itself. Behavioral scientists often consider "good rapport" as the sine qua non for "good research." It is an especially crucial dimension for anthropologists who are studying cultural groups that in some ways are very unlike their own. In these instances, anthropologists must be overtly sensitive to the customs and behavioral nuances of their own culture as well as that of their hosts.

I was aware, as were my two friends, that they were informing me about my own subculture as well as telling me about theirs, for anthropological rapport is a culturally symbiotic relationship. There must be a behavioral "fit" between the anthropologist and her or his informants for trust and understanding—essential ingredients in all anthropological research—to grow. If the anthropologist's behavior signifies a culturally antithetical persona, the wary informant will withdraw, and the research most certainly will flounder. So it is anthropologists as "cultural guests" who must make the accommodating moves if they want the approval and cooperation of informants.

Depending upon the society studied, these behavioral accommodations may take a variety of forms. For example, on my first research project I worked with college-educated Chinese from mainland China living in New York City (Hinkle et al. 1957). To gain their respect and establish rapport, I learned to sit much more quietly than was my usual wont and to ask personally sensitive questions indirectly. Fortunately, I already knew how to maintain a smile, as that too was important.

An even greater challenge to establishing behavioral rapport came on a field trip (Mitchell 1987) to Papua, New Guinea. Although American men generally avoid touching one another except for a ritual handshake or an occasional brusque slap on the back, men of the Wape tribe with whom I lived have a close physical relationship. Gathered together in the men's house, they visit amiably with legs intertwined and arms draped across each other's bodies, as if these were their own. And among the Iatmul, another New Guinea group I lived with, young men who are good friends sometimes stroll through the village holding hands by intertwining their little fingers. To the men of these societies such actions are commonplace, but for me they were emotionally charged. I was not aware of the affective strength behind the touching taboo of American males until I was in New Guinea and felt my personal space and body being "violated" by my new friends. My response was an almost overwhelming desire to pull away and draw myself in. Although I did not withdraw from their friendly touching and holding, it was only gradually that I learned to relax and enjoy their intimate camaraderie.

This account of fieldwork experiences may strike some as essentially trivial or inconsequential and not the critical factors in building rapport that I see them to be. Or some may view the anthropologist's behavioral adaptations to the host culture as contrived and manipulative. That would be unfortunate, because the motivation for "fitting in" goes far beyond the constraints of research methodology, important as this is. It also is intrinsically related to the strong humanist concern of anthropologists who spend years in the field augmenting their understanding of human nature, culture, and themselves. These behaviorally transforming fieldwork experiences serve the anthropologist as powerful entrees into the host culture. By adapting one's behavior to that of one's informants, a sense of empathy may be generated, and the work of learning the culture gets underway. This does not mean, however, that the anthropologist goes "native," nor am I espousing a "sentimental view of rapport as depending on the enfolding of anthropologist and informant into a single moral, emotional, and intellectual universe" that Clifford Geertz (1967:12) justly criticizes.

These personal fieldwork experiences are important because they help give the anthropologist a sense of the host culture and of its behavioral parameters. The field-worker begins to get the "feel" of the culture almost unwittingly as he or she succeeds in occasionally "fitting in" or receives a polite rebuke. Once, as a large group of New Guinea village children rushed onto our temporary and dangerously rickety porch, I called out loudly for them to get off. The children fled in terror. A nearby villager turned toward me and, his hushed voice filled with embarrassed anguish, said, "Speak gently!" My face burned with shame. But it was a lesson in Wape manners I never forgot.

This problem of how to communicate with one's informants and establish rapport in the field is an important methodological issue in modern anthropology.[2] "Communication"—or more properly in this context, "interpersonal communication"—specifically refers to face-to-face or two-way communication. It concerns the transmission of behavioral messages and how these messages are interpreted by others. In other words, the interpretation or "meaning" is separate from the act or "message." In this sense, communication is the process of creating a meaning from a message (Tubbs and Moss 1974:6). As my two Jewish friends had wisely advised me, the meaning my Jewish informants undoubtedly would give to my behavioral messages was, This man is a goy, beware!

When I joined the Jewish family research project I had little personal experience with Jewish-Gentile relations in American society. I did know that anti-Semitism was a chilling reality in American life and, as an anthropologist, I was certainly aware of the importance of cultural differences. But in my personal life I tended to play down ethnic differences among my friends and was impressed by the common humanity of New Yorkers amid such polyglot cultural diversity. So it came to me as a surprise when my two Jewish friends found my behavior and style of interaction so disturbingly different.

The social division between Gentiles and Jews is an ancient one, although what is meant by "gentile" depends upon the context. The term is from Latin and means "of the same clan or race." It formerly was used by Christians to refer to "heathens," is presently used by Mormons to refer to non-Mormons, and, of course, by Jews to refer to non-Jews, especially Christians. But here I will use the Yiddish term goy (goyim, pl.) to refer to the non-Jew, because it is a more culturally salient concept for the problem at hand.

While "gentile" is a somewhat neutral term, goy is loaded with cultural meaning stemming from the Jewish experience as a persecuted minority in the Diaspora. As used by Jews, it is a pejorative term, referring to someone who is "dull, insensitive, heartless." As Leo Rosten (1970:142) further points out in his discussion of the term, centuries of Jewish persecution have left a legacy of bitter sayings about goyim. For example, "Dos ken nor a goy," translated from the Yiddish, means "That, only a goy would do." Or the exclamation of exasperation "A goy!" is used "when endurance is exhausted, kindliness depleted, the effort to understand useless" (Rosten 1970:142).

It was during the research discussed here that I first became aware of the Jewish view of a distinct Jewish-Gentile cultural dichotomy characterized by the goy as a symbol of callousness and danger; the kind of person one tries to avoid if possible. As my informants led me into their perceptual world, I too, albeit reluctantly, began to see individuals in terms of this dichotomy. I was so deeply imprinted with this ethnic duality during the research experience that it has been one of the most enduring personal effects of the study. Learning firsthand about the inexorableness of ethnic divisions was an emotionally powerful experience because it challenged and in some ways shattered my youthful "one world" idealism. An early response is recorded in my notebook:

This family circle meeting was the first time I was accosted with a Jewish-Gentile dichotomy. It was presented to me in several quite personal ways. Some pleasant and some joking; others that were to me of a negative tinge. Aunt Edith, who is 50, kept coming up to me and telling me how fine the Jews were, that the Jews and Gentiles should learn to get together, that the Jews want to get along with the Gentiles, that most Jews are fine people like here at the family circle, all Jews want is to be friends with the Gentiles, isn't it a shame the way the Jews are sometimes treated, etc. I was quite amazed by all of this talk and even more at a loss as to how to handle the indomitable interaction entrances. It all seemed quite irrelevant, and it annoyed me that I was being accepted— provisionally— as a "good" Gentile rather than as a fellow human being.

In my research with other cultural groups—college-educated Chinese and Papua New Guineans, for example—it was obvious that I was an outsider because of my light skin color, but with my Jewish informants the situation was not as clear. Racially we were Caucasians, but culturally there were significant differences.[3] While I doubt that any of my informants seriously believed I was Jewish, it still was very important to them that they be absolutely sure. They knew that the research was sponsored in part by a Jewish social work agency and that we were studying Jewish family-kin relationships. Their underlying question seemed to be, What's he here for if he's not Jewish?

During the interviews at the beginning of the research, an informant would usually pause at some point and, eyebrows raised, diffidently ask, "You Jewish?" During one interview, an informant's elderly mother came into the room and, after listening to our conversation for a while, asked the inevitable question. When I said "No," she shook her head sagely and replied with a strong Yiddish accent, "You don't look Jewish!" The point is that unambiguous ethnic identification of me was of great importance to my informants. They needed to know if I was an "insider" or an "outsider"—did I "belong" or didn't I.

So I learned to volunteer during the first meeting that I was not Jewish and to offer other personal information about myself. While the New Guinea Wape were singularly disinterested in my cultural background, my Jewish informants seemed pleased when I gave them information placing me in a specific social context. Instead of waiting to be pumped for personal data, I could always count on an amused expression, for example, when I volunteered that I was born and raised in Wichita, Kansas.

In some of the Jewish homes that I visited, I was something of an "event" because I was the first goy guest. Many of my informants lived in an almost entirely Jewish world—socially if not physically ghettoized—in terms of significant relationships with their neighbors, fellow workers, friends, and, of course, relatives. This is possible in a city with several million Jews where large sections of the city and even certain industries have become predominantly Jewish in composition. For persons who have spent most of their lives in an almost totally Jewish milieu, social relations with goyim are unusual and, when they do occur, are touched with apprehension. After a pleasant visit with a Jewish family accompanied by an informant, I learned that I was the first "Wasp" to have entered the home. My informant's comment about our hostess was, "I bet she gave a sigh of relief when you went out the door!"

This sort of apprehensiveness was reflected in most of my initial interviews with informant families. There was always some hesitation on my first visit, a kind of cautious stiffness that I interpreted as misgivings, perhaps even overt suspiciousness. But that mood was never sustained. I found that the best way to break it was to begin collecting a genealogy as soon as possible. As we set to work on the family's genealogy with brown wrapping paper spread out on the kitchen table and usually a soft drink and cookies on the side, the tension would subside. Most of my informants became intensely engrossed in watching the social and cultural dimensions of their family network unfold before their eyes. "My," one woman exclaimed with enthusiasm, "isn't this interesting!"

However, there was always a certain amount of bemusement that I, a goy, was studying Jews. There was something wrong—intrusive maybe—about this goy, this outsider, trying to get "inside" Jewish family life. This "wonderment" regarding my involvement in the research project was expressed to me primarily via joking comments. Not only did my informants seem a bit muddled and amused about my research role, but so did my New York Jewish friends and colleagues. At the time, I did not know how to interpret this levity;

I know I failed to see the humor to the extent they did. For me it was a serious and fascinating research project and my involvement did not strike me as odd or "funny." I could not help but feel that the smiles and laughter were tinged with disapproval, that the joking response was covering up at least some resentment towards this presumptuous goy who was trying to penetrate Jewish family life.

But once I was accepted, family members went out of their way to make me feel as though I were not the comparative stranger that I obviously was. Still, there were often problems if my informant had to go beyond the immediate family to get information or to grant me permission to attend a specific family function. There was then a need for the inevitable explanation of who I was and why did I want what I wanted. Sometimes the explanations didn't make much sense to older family members whose suspicions about the goyim had been documented, not just by social discrimination and negative insinuations, but by horrifying personal experiences in Eastern Europe and the genocidal murder of close relatives.

Because of my own idealism regarding intergroup interactions and because I was an "integrated" member of a Jewish social agency, I at first was unaware of any emotional connection between the Holocaust and my research role. I could remember as an impressionable teenager photos and newsreels of the German concentration camps and the terrifying impact they had upon me, so it never occurred to me that such heinous events could be associated, even remotely, with my research. I can recall the sickening feeling I had when a male informant during the last week of interviewing wisecracked that I was collecting Jewish genealogies for "a giant Manhattan concentration camp." I laughed, but I was so struck by the monstrousness of the comment that I wrote it down. I was puzzled how a man of my own age and American-born could bring such a macabre association to my research. Then three days later while interviewing another informant, the "concentration camp" image appeared again. I wrote in my notebook: "[My informant] said that he had asked his uncle, who is president of their Family Circle, for the documents and explained what I was doing. The uncle was skeptical and joked about my collecting all of the family names for a concentration camp. [My informant] said it was doubtful if he could get the documents for me."

The goyim issue was a pervasive problem that influenced all of my informant relationships. Establishing rapport undoubtedly would have been easier if I were a Jew but, as an outsider, I was able to see some things more clearly and with less distorting personal involvement than could a member of the group.[4] However, there were other problems less specifically ethnic in origin that in some instances also affected my relationships with informants.

Informant disapproval is not a unique response to anthropological research, especially in literate societies. To be "studied" is seen by some as demeaning; that one is being treated as an object rather than as a person. I occasionally ran into this type of resistance, especially when I tried to gain access to family social events and was turned away because some family members didn't want to be "studied." Family affairs, including meetings of family clubs, were generally considered private activities where relatives could relax and have fun. The presence of a researcher, I was once told, would put "a damper" on the festivities.[5]

There was also the problem of the popular view that anthropologists are primarily interested in "primitive peoples," hardly a flattering notion to a "civilized" person whose group has attracted anthropological interest. "A sociologist," said one informant, "I can understand, but why an anthropologist?"[6] Morton Fried (1959:351) faced a similar problem when, on beginning his anthropological fieldwork in east-central China, he was summoned to appear at the office of the county magistrate. "The magistrate was polite but cold: an anthropological study of his country was an affront; anthropologists, said the magistrate, studied only savages and barbarians."

There are, however, communication problems other than those directly related to informant rapport that have an impact upon the research process and the anthropologist's understanding of what is happening. Among these is how the anthropologist interprets an informant's "interaction style"; that is, the culturally patterned actions that characterize how a person initiates and/or responds to others. The anthropologist, like all other human beings, is culturally trained from infancy to interpret and respond to the behavioral patterns of her or his own culture in a specific and often unconscious way. When working in another culture, therefore, the anthropologist is always at risk of projecting a behavioral interpretation from his or her own culture onto the one being studied.

Anthropologists call this phenomenon "ethnocentrism" and recognize it as a common cause of distortion and misunderstanding among individuals of diverse ethnic backgrounds. Although a behavioral act in two different cultures may appear to be the same, the social meanings of the act can vary; what looks like one thing in one's own culture may have a very different meaning in the host culture. During the first months of the research as I was learning about the culture and its characteristic interaction style, I frequently misinterpreted an informant's behavior.

Initially, I was somewhat abashed by my informants' familiarity and verbal frankness. As a group they were quick to express their personal views, even very negative ones, about their relatives and family affairs. Their extreme candor about "family skeletons," as well as their boasting about family accomplishments, occasionally embarrassed me. I was unaccustomed to such bold forthrightness—it was almost the reverse of my own subculture and the Chinese I had studied. And, while I might marvel at their unreserved and seemingly uncensored presentation of themselves and their families, I wondered how family members could endure such brashness without alienating one another.

Although they treated me kindly as a guest in their home, these informants felt no constraint to defer to me politely as my Chinese informants had done. If I made some passing, and to me, innocuous comment, I might be challenged directly with an opposing view. If they thought I had misunderstood or not comprehended a point in the interview, they would abruptly correct me or ruefully continue their explanation. They were excellent informants, willing to instruct me in details but ever ready to chide me if they thought I didn't understand completely. Most of them quickly grasped the nature of my study, even anticipating my next question and volunteering information before I had the presence of mind to ask for it. It was exciting research, fast paced and fully developed, but it wasn't what I would call "easy." It demanded a great deal of mental discipline because the data and its nuances appeared so rapidly. It was very different from later work with the New Guinea Lujere (Mitchell 1977) when some of my informant interviews moved so slowly that I could occasionally daydream about home and still keep track of what was being said in a foreign language.

But there was no time to daydream with my Jewish informants. I was too busy keeping abreast of the interview action. At first, I tended to misinterpret their avid outspokenness and abrupt corrections and comments as "put-downs" of myself. It seemed as if I could do nothing right and that nothing was sacred; if they had a view it existed to be expressed. Even my own cultural background did not escape critical commentary. Once, in an interview on Jewish weddings, I commented that the giving of money as a wedding gift was different from my family's custom:

MRS. X: Well, you are not Jewish, or no?
WM: No.
MRS. X: No, then that's the difference. The style is entirely different! I know in your case they usually bring gifts in their display.
WM: That's right.
MRS. X: And everyone brings a piece of junk, and by the time you get through, half that stuff is thrown out. You don't even use it. Am I right?

This kind of critical forthrightness, to my chagrin, sometimes would throw me off balance. However, as I learned not to withdraw—for that only made the interviewee more impatient and anxious—my interviews became both more interesting and valuable. My informants seemed more comfortable because they had someone to "push" against or disagree with. I also learned that it wasn't really important for us to agree; no one had to "win." It was the disputation or "status jockeying" that was important; it made the interaction sequence exciting and, I can't help but thinking now, not blandly goyish.

Learning this disputatious interaction style was a challenge because it was different from my own more circumspect cultural style in which one should protect the feelings of the other person, and open disagreements, especially with relative strangers, are avoided. There is, however, a special exhilaration in the disputatious style. It is bold and assertive and intellectually stimulating. One must think quickly to marshall evidence for a convincing riposte. What once would have seemed like an inappropriate argument came to feel like a stimulating discussion about a disagreement. Later, when I asked an informant about conflicts or arguments with respect to her family circle organization, I knew exactly what she meant when she smilingly replied, "Oh, we don't have arguments! We have disagreements!" Nevertheless, because a disputatious interaction style is concerned with interpersonal conflict, it flirts with danger. A lively discussion may easily move into genuine quarreling if a participant "pushes" too hard, is too intractable, or is insulting.[7]

Related to this assertive interaction style is the phenomenon of "overtalking"—two or more individuals speaking simultaneously. Again, this was different from my own subculture where it is considered either "rude" or "aggressive" to speak when another person is talking. To keep from losing control of an interview when my informant interrupted me, I learned how to "overtalk" by raising my voice as I persisted in asking a question or making a comment; however, I never succeeded in feeling at ease with this tactic. The problem was even more difficult when I did a family interview with parents and children. Verbatim transcriptions of these interviews presented a complex methodological problem when, for example, the wife, husband, teen-age daughter, and I were each competing verbally for attention.

In an important way, this chapter is about language—language in its widest application to include the symbolic display of both the voice and the body. I have emphasized the differences between Gentiles and Jews in these communicative displays as exemplified by my experience as an anthropologist studying New York City Jewish families of Eastern European ethnic background. It is an anthropological truism that one's culture helps to shape how we perceive ourselves and others. It is also true that intimate experience with another culture can affect one's perceptions and understanding. In the Jewish research, I learned that I was a goy, a pejorative term signifying that I was a callous outsider and potential enemy. My physical appearance and style of interaction further corroborated the cultural differences between my informants and me. These were facts embedded in deep and compelling cultural histories. Nothing I might do could completely change or transcend them.

There is an old Yiddish saying, "A goy bleibt a goy!" that translates loosely as, "Once a goy, always a goy!" I was a goy, but in my role as an anthropologist, I made a concerted attempt to modify my goyisher kop, my "Gentile ways." By consciously working to accommodate my behavior and interaction style to that of my Jewish informants, I was able to feel my way into this host culture and gradually develop a sense of empathy and "connectedness" that facilitated the communication process. Although I never completely attained the easy verbal and gestural expressiveness of my Jewish informants (or, for that matter, the easy physical intimacy of my Wape male informants), I did achieve an approximation that made me feel and look less behaviorally foreign. And once I understood that my informants' disputatious interaction style was not a personal attack but an elaborated form of provocative play, I could enter into the exchange without fear of hurting someone's feelings or suffering a damaged ego myself.

At the end of the project I moved to northern Vermont to work with rural and village families and encountered yet another problem in cultural adaption. Compared to the placid mien of many rural Vermont Yankee males, my indigenous Kansas style of interaction was rather lively and when augmented by the expressive behaviors learned during the

Jewish project, it became explosively dynamic. My wife, a native Vermonter, admonished me to modify my interaction style. There it was the "village idiot," not the successful man, who cultivated verbal and behavioral expressiveness.

Communication problems are a "given" of anthropological fieldwork. The nature of the problems and how they are revealed depends partly upon the culture of the anthropologist and the culture of the informant. To what extent the anthropologist is successful in adapting his or her behavior patterns to those of the host culture will vary greatly. It is a problem area that has had little, if any, formal discussion among anthropologists, although it is a crucial dimension of fieldwork that may have an enduring effect on the anthropologist's life. Each group with whom an anthropologist works, if one is sensitive to the kinds of communication problems explored here, helps to change and/or augment one's behavioral repertoire. In this sense, fieldwork research is a transforming experience.

My research with New York City Jewish families was no exception. Like most anthropological fieldwork, it has had a lasting influence upon me. Encountering the profound rigidity of ethnic divisions was, in spite of my Kansas optimism, a disillusioning experience. Nevertheless, my personal life has been enriched by learning a lively cultural style of interaction quite different from my own. Perhaps of even more significance, I learned something known by members of this culture for many centuries: how it feels to be a dangerous outsider.

NOTES

For comments on a draft of this paper, I am grateful to Jack Kugelmass, Annette B. Weiner, and Jonathan B. Weiner.

1. The parent project was cosponsored by the Jewish Family Service of New York and the Russell Sage Foundation. The project was directed by Hope Jensen Leichter, and the regular research staff included Fred Davis, Judith Lieb, Alice Liu Szema, Dianne Tendler, Candace Rogers, and myself. A detailed account of the samples, methodology, and findings of this study are reported in Leichter and Mitchell (1978). For similar information on the study of Jewish family clubs, see Mitchell (1980). The majority of the data for both studies was collected between 1958 and 1962.

2. See, e.g., Freilich (1970); Hammersley and Atkinson (1983); Lawless, Sutlive, and Zamora (1983); Mead (1970); and Pelto and Pelto (1973). More recently, some anthropologists, e.g., Marcus and Fischer (1986), Ruby (1982), and Stocking (1983), have developed a critical interest in the anthropologist's fieldwork experience in a particular society and how this is reflected in resulting publications.

3. Although Jews are sometimes collectively called "the Jewish race," this is scientifically incorrect. Race is a biological concept. There is great variation among Jews in terms of physical characteristics, and this disqualifies them from being a race per se. On this subject, see Newman (1965:21–30) and Shapiro (1960).

4. For example, even Jewish social scientists who were members of a "family circle" or "cousins' club" did not recognize the uniqueness of these urban descent groups in the ethnographic record or their importance for kinship theory but tended to react to them as annoyances that demanded an occasional appearance at a meeting or special event.

5. This negative response to anthropological research has become a frequent response in the Third World, where anthropologists are sometimes viewed as having been handmaidens to an exploitative colonialism and are now barred from doing fieldwork in some countries. See, e.g., Strathern (1983).

6. It is true that it is very unusual for a Gentile to study and publish on Jewish life. As Mayer (1973:152) has noted, "the sociology of Jews has been written almost exclusively by Jews."

7. For substantive data on conflict among Jews of Eastern European descent and its cultural background see Leichter and Mitchell (1978:166–184); Mitchell (1978:155–168); and Zborowski and Herzog (1952).

REFERENCES

Freilich, Morris, ed. 1970. *Marginal Natives: Anthropologists at Work.* New York: Harper & Row.

Fried, Morton H. 1959. *Readings in Anthropology,* vol. 2. New York: Thomas Y. Crowell.

Geertz, Clifford. 1967. "Under the Mosquito Net." *New York Review of Books* 9:12–13.

Hammersley, Martyn, and Paul Atkinson. 1983. *Ethnography: Principles in Practice.* London: Tavistock.

Hinkel, Lawrence, et al. 1957. "Factors Relevant to the Occurrence of Bodily Illness and Disturbances in Mood, Thought and Behavior in Three Homogeneous Population Groups." *American Journal of Psychiatry* 114:212–20.

Lawless, Robert, Vincent H. Sutlive, Jr., and Mario D. Zamora, eds. 1983. *Fieldwork: The Human Experience.* New York: Gordon and Breach.

Leichter, Hope Jensen, and William E. Mitchell. 1978. *Kinship and Casework: Family Networks and Social Intervention.* New York: Teachers College Press.

Marcus, George E., and Michael M. J. Fischer. 1986. *Anthropology as Cultural Critique: An Experimental Moment in the Human Sciences.* Chicago: University of Chicago Press.

Mayer, Egon. 1973. "Jewish Orthodoxy in America: Towards the Sociology of a Residual Category." *Jewish Journal of Sociology* 15:151–65.

Mead, Margaret. 1970. "The Art and Technique of Fieldwork," in *Handbook of Method in Cultural Anthropology,* Raoul Naroll and Ronald Cohen, eds. New York: Columbia University Press.

Mitchell, William E. 1977. "Sorcellerie chamanique: Sanguma chez lez Lujere du cours supérieur de Sépik." *Journal de la Société des Océanistes* 33:178–89.

———. 1980. *Mishpokhe: A Study of New York City Jewish Family Clubs,* 2nd ed. Hawthorne, N.Y.: Aldine.

———. 1987. *The Bamboo Fire: Field Work with the New Guinea Wape,* 2nd ed. Prospect Heights, Ill.: Waveland Press.

Newman, Louis I. 1965. *The Jewish People, Faith and Life.* New York: Bloch.

Pelto, Pertti J., and Gretel H. Pelto. 1973. "Ethnography: The Fieldwork Enterprise," in *Handbook of Social and Cultural Anthropology,* John J. Honigmann, ed. Chicago: Rand McNally.

Rosten, Leo. 1970. *The Joys of Yiddish.* New York: Simon and Schuster.

Ruby, Jay, ed. 1982. *A Crack in the Mirror: Reflexive Perspectives in Anthropology.* Philadelphia: University of Pennsylvania Press.

Shapiro, Harry I. 1960. *The Jewish People: A Biological History.* Paris: UNESCO.

Stocking, George W. Jr., ed. 1983. *Observers Observed: Essays on Ethnographic Fieldwork.* Madison: University of Wisconsin Press.

Strathern, Andrew. 1983. "Research in Papua New Guinea: Cross-Currents of Conflict." *Royal Anthropological Institute News,* no. 58:4–10.

Tubbs, Stewart L., and Sylvia Moss. 1974. *Human Communication: An Interpersonal Perspective.* New York: Random House.

Zborowski, Mark, and Elizabeth Herzog. 1952. *Life Is with People: The Culture of the Shtetl.* New York: International Universities Press.

◆ WRITING/DISCUSSION EXERCISES

1.1   Read William E. Mitchell's "A Goy in the Ghetto." Write a short summary of the article, focusing on how he describes his fieldwork experiences and the adjustments in communicative style that he needed to make in each setting.

1.2   List at least five different examples of how linguistic anthropology overlaps with one other subfield of anthropology.

1.3   Briefly describe one example of an overlap (or mutual area of interest) between linguistic anthropology and one other subfield of anthropology and develop a list of references (books, journal articles, magazine articles, websites) where you can find more information about it.

1.4   Describe one way in which an understanding of language structure or context might contribute to your own major field of study.

WEB EXERCISES

1.1 Follow the links on the companion website about anthropology in the field. In particular look for examples of anthropologists writing about their field experiences. When you find an appropriate link, write a short summary of that anthropologist's challenges in getting to the field, learning the language, getting adjusted, and shifting frames of reference. Discuss your summary with others in the class.

1.2 Follow the link on the companion website to the American Anthropological Association's statement on ethics in anthropology. Summarize some of the ways that the statement addresses the dictum "Do no harm." Compare your understanding of this dictum with that of others in your class.

1.3   Search the InfoTrac database for articles about fieldwork in cultural and linguistic anthropology.

1.4   Search the InfoTrac database for articles about Franz Boas and the beginnings of linguistic anthropology in the United States.

GUIDED PROJECTS

Language Creating

This is a semester-long project in which you will create an actual language. You will do this with a group of your classmates. Your instructor will provide you with the information that you need for each step of the project. The project will assist you in learning more about the structure of language and how language is used in everyday life. It will also help you to understand more about how languages are invented for use in movies and novels.

If your instructor has assigned this project, then this is the time to form your language-creating group. Your group should have between four and six individuals. Give your group a name if you wish. Exchange contact information (e-mail addresses, phone numbers) with everyone in your group. Give your instructor a list of all the members of your group. If your group has a name, then give that to your instructor as well, or be prepared for your instructor to give your group a name.

Conversation Partnering

This is a semester-long project in which you will serve as a "conversation partner" for a student whose first language is different from yours. You will be expected to meet with this person on a weekly basis. Because we understand that each of you will probably already be quite busy, we encourage you to do things with your conversation partner that do not disrupt your schedules. Consider eating lunch together, going to movies together, going shopping together, or even studying together. Just be sure to spend at least some of your time together exploring similarities and differences between your two languages. Your instructor will provide you with specific exercises that can guide you through these cross-language comparisons. The comparisons will assist you with learning and applying specific concepts and skills. They will also help you to learn more about each other's language. By the end of the semester you will not only discover that you have learned a lot about languages from this experience, but you will probably also have found a new friend.

If your instructor has assigned this project, this is the time to get matched up with a conversation partner. Your instructor will provide you with more details on how to do this. Be prepared to give your instructor information on your schedule and interests so that you can be matched with a compatible partner. If you already have a conversation partner or have a friend, roommate, or co-worker whose first language is different from your own and who is willing to serve as your conversation partner for the purposes of this project, then you should notify your instructor immediately.

CHAPTER 2

Language and Culture

Note: Your instructor will indicate which readings, exercises, and/or projects you should do.

✳ READING

2.0 "Hanunóo Color Categories" by Harold C. Conklin

Harold Conklin's "Hanunóo Color Categories" is a classic in the field of linguistic anthropology. It shows how different languages divide the world of color in different ways, but it also shows how the associations for each color range may be different in different languages. This is one of the early articles published in the field of cognitive anthropology; it helped pave the way for the development of that approach to understanding worldview and categorization through language. (Conklin's field work among the Hanunóo on Mindoro Island (1952–1954) was supported by grants from the Social Science Research Council, the Ford Foundation, and the Guggenheim Foundation.)

In the following brief analysis of a specific Philippine color system I shall attempt to show how various ethnographic field techniques may be combined profitably in the study of lexical sets relating to perceptual categorization.

Recently, I completed more than a year's field research on Hanunóo folkbotany.[1] In this type of work one soon becomes acutely aware of problems connected with understanding the local system of color categorization because plant determinations so often depend on chromatic differences in the appearance of flowers or vegetative structures—both in taxonomic botany and in popular systems of classification. It is no accident that one of the most detailed accounts of native color terminology in the Malayo-Polynesian area was written by a botanist.[2] I was, therefore, greatly concerned with Hanunóo color categories during the entire period of my ethnobotanical research. Before summarizing the specific results of my analysis of the Hanunóo material, however, I should like to draw attention to several general considerations.

1. Color, in a western technical sense, is not a universal concept and in many languages such as Hanunóo there is no unitary terminological equivalent. In our technical literature definitions state that color is the evaluation of the visual sense of that quality of light (reflected or transmitted by some substance) which is basically determined by its spectral composition. The spectrum is the range of visible color in light measured in wave lengths (400 [deep red] to 700 [blue-violet] millimicrons).[3] The total color sphere—holding any set of external and surface conditions constant—includes two other dimensions, in addition to that of spectral position or hue. One is saturation or intensity (chroma), the other brightness or brilliance (value). These three perceptual dimensions are usually combined into a coordinate system as a cylindrical continuum known as the color solid. Saturation diminishes toward the central axis which forms the achromatic core of neutral grays from the white at the end of greatest brightness to black at the opposite extremity. Hue varies with

Source: "Hanunóo Color Categories," by Harold C. Conklin. *Southwestern Journal of Anthropology* 11(4): 339–344. Copyright © 1955 The Journal of Anthropological Research. Reprinted by permission.

circumferential position. Although technically speaking *black* is the absence of any "color," *white,* the presence of all visible color wave lengths, and neutral *grays* lack spectral distinction, these achromatic positions within the color solid are often included with spectrally-defined positions in the categories distinguished in popular color systems.

2. Under laboratory conditions, color *discrimination* is probably the same for all human populations, irrespective of language; but the manner in which different languages classify the millions[4] of "colors" which every normal individual can discriminate *differ.* Many stimuli are classified as equivalent, as extensive, cognitive—or perceptual—screening takes place.[5] Requirements of specification may differ considerably from one culturally-defined situation to another. The largest collection[6] of English color names runs to over 3,000 entries, yet only eight of these occur very commonly.[7] Recent testing by Lenneberg and others[8] demonstrates a high correlation in English and in Zuñi between ready color vocabulary and *ease in recognition of colors.* Although this is only a beginning it does show how the structure of a lexical set may affect color perception. It may also be possible to determine certain nonlinguistic correlates for color terminology. Color terms are a part of the vocabulary of particular languages and only the intracultural analysis of such lexical sets and their correlates can provide the key to their understanding and range of applicability. The study of isolated and assumed translations in other languages can lead only to confusion.[9]

In the field I began to investigate Hanunóo color classification in a number of ways, including the eliciting of linguistic responses from a large number of informants to painted cards, dyed fabrics, other previously prepared materials,[10] and the recording of visual-quality attributes taken from descriptions of specific items of the natural and artificial surroundings. This resulted in the collection of a profusion of attributive words of the non-formal—and therefore in a sense "color"—type. There were at first many inconsistencies and a high degree of overlap for which the controls used did not seem to account. However, as the work with plant specimens and minute floristic differentiation progressed, I noted that in *contrastive* situations this initial confusion and incongruity of informants' responses did not usually occur. In such situations, where the "nonformal (i.e., not spatially organized) visible quality"[11] of one substance (plant part, dyed thread, or color card) was to be related to and contrasted with that of another, both of which were either at hand or well known, terminological agreement was reached with relative ease. Such a defined situation seemed to provide the frame necessary for establishing a known level of specification. Where needed, a greater degree of specification (often employing different root morphemes) could be and was made. Otherwise, such finer distinctions were ignored. This hint of terminologically significant levels led to a reexamination of all color data and the following analysis emerged.

Color distinctions in Hanunóo are made at two levels of contrast. The first, higher, more general level consists of an all-inclusive, coordinate, four-way classification which lies at the core of the color system. The four categories are mutually exclusive in contrastive contexts, but may overlap slightly in absolute (i.e., spectrally, or in other measurable) terms. The second level, including several sublevels, consists of hundreds of specific color categories, many of which overlap and interdigitate. Terminologically, there is "unanimous agreement"[12] on the designations for the four Level I categories, but considerable lack of unanimity—with a few explainable exceptions—in the use of terms at Level II.

The four Level I terms are:

1. (ma) bīru[13] 'relative darkness (of shade of color); blackness' (black)
2. (ma)lagti? 'relative lightness (or tint of color); whiteness' (white)
3. (ma)rara? 'relative presence of red; redness' (red)
4. (ma)latuy 'relative presence of light greenness; greenness' (green)

The three-dimensional color solid is divided by this Level I categorization into four unequal parts; the largest is *mabīru,* the smallest *malatuy.* While boundaries separating these categories cannot be set in absolute terms, the focal points (differing slightly in size, themselves) within the four sections, can be limited more or less to black, white, orange-red, and leaf-green respectively. In general terms, *mabīru* includes the range usually covered in English by black, violet, indigo, blue, dark green, dark gray, and deep shades of other colors and mixtures; *malagti⁷,* white and very light tints of other colors and mixtures; *marara⁷,* maroon, red, orange, yellow, and mixtures in which these qualities are seen to predominate; *malatuy,* light green, and mixtures of green, yellow, and light brown. All color terms can be reduced to one of these four but none of the four is reducible. This does not mean that other color terms are synonyms, but that they designate color categories of greater specification within four recognized color realms.

The basis of this Level I classification appears to have certain correlates beyond what is usually considered the range of chromatic differentiation, and which are associated with nonlinguistic phenomena in the external environment. First, there is the opposition between light and dark, obvious in the contrasted ranges of meaning of *lagti⁷* and *bīru.* Second, there is an opposition between dryness or desiccation and wetness or freshness (succulence) in visible components of the natural environment which are reflected in the terms *rara⁷* and *latuy* respectively. This distinction is of particular significance in terms of plant life. Almost all living plant types possess some fresh, succulent, and often "greenish" parts. To eat any kind of raw, uncooked food, particularly fresh fruits or vegetables, is known as *pag-laty-un* (< *latuy*). A shiny, wet, *brown*-colored section of newly-cut bamboo is *malatuy* (not *marara⁷*). Dried-out or matured plant material such as certain kinds of yellowed bamboo or hardened kernels of mature or parched corn are *marara⁷.* To become desiccated, to lose all moisture, is known as *mamara⁷* (< *para⁷* 'desiccation'; and parenthetically, I might add that there are morphological and historical reasons—aside from Hanunóo folk etymologizing—to believe that at least the final syllables of these two forms are derived from a common root). A third opposition, dividing the two already suggested, is that of deep, unfading, indelible, and hence often more desired material as against pale, weak, faded, bleached, or "colorless" substance, a distinction contrasting *mabīru* and *marara⁷* with *malagti⁷* and *malatuy.* This opposition holds for manufactured items and trade goods as well as for some natural products (e.g., red and white trade beads, red being more valuable by Hanunóo standards; indigo-dyed cotton sarongs, the most prized being those dyed most often and hence of the deepest indigo color—sometimes obscuring completely the designs formed originally by *white* warp yarns; etc.). Within each of these Level I categories, increased esthetic value attaches as the focal points mentioned above are approached. There is only one exception: the color which is most tangibly visible in their jungle surroundings, the green (even the focal point near light- or yellow-green) of the natural vegetation, is not valued decoratively. Green beads, for example, are "unattractive," worthless. Clothing and ornament are valued in proportion to the sharpness of contrast between, and the intensity (lack of mixture, deep quality) of "black," "red," and "white."

Level II terminology is normally employed only when greater specification than is possible at Level I is required, or when the name of an object referred to happens also to be a "color" term (e.g., *bulāwan* 'gold; golden [color]'). Level II terms are of two kinds: relatively specific color words like *(ma)dapug* 'gray' (< *dapug* 'hearth; ashes'), *(ma)⁷arum* 'violet,' *(ma)dilaw* 'yellow' (< *dilaw* 'turmeric'); and constructions, based on such specific terms— or on Level I names—but involving further derivations, such as *mabirubiru* 'somewhat *mabīru*' (more specific than *mabīru* alone only in that a color which is *not* a solid, deep, black is implied, i.e., a color classed within the *mabīru* category at Level 1, but not at or near the focal point), *mabiiru (gid)* 'very *mabīru*' (here something close to the focal center of jet black is designated), and *madīlawdīlaw* 'weak yellow.' Much attention is paid to the texture of the surface referred to, the resulting degree and type of reflection (iridescent, sparkling, dull), and to admixture of other nonformal qualities. Frequently these noncolorimetric aspects are considered of primary importance, the more spectrally-definable qualities serving only as secondary attributes. In either case polymorphemic descriptions are common.

At Level II there is a noticeable difference in the ready color vocabulary of men as compared to women. The former excel (in the degree of specification to which they carry such classification terminologically) in the ranges of "reds" and "grays" (animals, hair, feather, etc.); the latter, in "blues" (shades of indigo-dyed fabrics). No discernible similar difference holds for the "greens" or "whites."

In short, we have seen that the apparent complexity of the Hanunóo color system can be reduced at the most generalized level to four basic terms which are associated with lightness, darkness, wetness, and dryness. This intracultural analysis demonstrates that what appears to be color "confusion" at first may result from an inadequate knowledge of the internal structure of a color system and from a failure to distinguish sharply between sensory reception on the one hand and perceptual categorization on the other.

NOTES

1. Conklin, 1954a, 1954b.
2. Bartlett, 1929.
3. Osgood, 1953, p. 137.
4. Estimates range from 7,500,000 to more than 10,000,000 (Optical Society of America, 1953; Evans, 1948, p. 230).
5. Lounsbury, 1953.
6. Maerz and Paul, 1930.
7. Thorndike and Lorge, 1944.
8. Lenneberg, 1953, pp. 468–471; Lenneberg and Roberts, 1954; Brown and Lenneberg, 1954.
9. Lenneberg, 1953, pp. 464–466; Hjelmslev, 1953, p. 33.
10. Cf. Ray, 1952, 1953.

11. The lack of a term similar in semantic range to our word "color" makes abstract interrogation in Hanunóo about such matters somewhat complicated. Except for leading questions (naming some visual-quality attribute as a possibility), only circumlocutions such as *kabitay tīda nu pagbantāyun?* 'How is it to look at?' are possible. If this results in description of spatial organization or form, the inquiry may be narrowed by the specification *bukun kay ʔanyuʔ* 'not its shape (or form).'
12. Lenneberg, 1953, p. 469.
13. These forms occur as attributes with the prefix *ma-* 'exhibiting, having,' as indicated above in parentheses, or as free words (abstracts).

BIBLIOGRAPHY

Bartlett, Harley Harris. 1929. Color Nomenclature in Batak and Malay. *Papers, Michigan Academy of Science, Arts and Letters*, vol. 10, pp. 1–52, Ann Arbor.

Brown, Roger W., and Eric H. Lenneberg. 1954. A Study in Language and Cognition. *Journal of Abnormal and Social Psychology*, vol. 49, pp. 454–462.

Conklin, Harold C. 1954a. *The Relation of Hanunóo Culture to the Plant World*. Doctoral dissertation, Yale University, New Haven.

———. 1954b. An Ethnoecological Approach to Shifting Agriculture. *Transactions, New York Academy of Sciences*, ser. II, vol. 17, pp. 133–142, New York.

Evans, Ralph M. 1948. *An Introduction to Color*. New York: Wiley.

Hjelmslev, Louis. 1953. *Prolegomena to a Theory of Language*. Indiana University Publications in Anthropology and Linguistics, Memoir 7 of the International Journal of American Linguistics [translated by Francis J. Whitfield], Bloomington.

Lenneberg, Eric H. 1953. Cognition in Ethnolinguistics. *Language*, vol. 29, pp. 463–471, Baltimore.

Lenneberg, Eric H., and John M. Roberts. 1954. *The Language of Experience, a Case Study*. Communications Program, Center of International Studies, Massachusetts Institute of Technology, Cambridge: hectographed, 45 pp. and 9 figs.

Lounsbury, Floyd G. 1953. "Introduction" [section on Linguistics and Psychology] (In *Results of the Conference of Anthropologists and Linguists*, pp. 47–49, Memoir 8, International Journal of American Linguistics, Baltimore).

Maerz, A., and M. R. Paul. 1930. *A Dictionary of Color*. New York: McGraw-Hill.

Optical Society of America, Committee on Colorimetry. 1953. *The Science of Color.* New York: Crowell.

Osgood, Charles E. 1953. *Method and Theory in Experimental Psychology.* New York: Oxford University Press.

Ray, Verne F. 1952. Techniques and Problems in the Study of Human Color Perception. *Southwestern Journal of Anthropology,* vol. 8, pp. 251–259.

————. 1953. Human Color Perception and Behavioral Response. *Transactions, New York Academy of Sciences,* ser. II, vol. 16, pp. 98–104, New York.

Thorndike, E. L., and I. Lorge. 1944. *The Teacher's Word Book of 30,000 Words.* New York: Teacher's College, Columbia University.

 # WRITING/DISCUSSION EXERCISES

2.1   Read Conklin's "Hanunóo Color Categories." Write a short summary of the article, focusing on how Conklin used ethnosemantic analysis to reveal the underlying system of the Hanunóo color naming system. Be prepared to discuss your summary with your classmates.

2.2   Write a short summary of Conklin's "Hanunóo Color Categories," focusing on the way that the Hanunóo color naming system reflects Hanunóo cultural emphasis. Discuss the relationship between naming systems and cultural emphasis with your classmates.

2.3 What does Conklin's article suggest about the relationship of Hanunóo culture to the plant world?

2.4 Give an example of an area for which you have a complex range of words. How does this reflect your interests? The culture in which you grew up?

2.5 Ethnosemantics: Pair up with a friend or classmate and do ethnosemantic research with one another. Investigate words for drinks, foods, fishing, or whatever seems to be interesting and relevant. Prepare a taxonomy and a componential analysis for each semantic domain that you research. One goal of this exercise is to learn something about someone else's categorization system. Another is to experience what it feels like to have someone else explore your categorization system. An overall goal is to gain familiarity with some of the basics of ethnosemantic fieldwork.

First you will each need to select a semantic domain or area of cultural emphasis that you will research. Have a conversation to find out what each of you is most interested in (consider hobbies, work, and studies). One good way to identify a semantic domain is to ask a "Grand Tour" kind of question, like "Tell me about a typical day," and then to listen for something that sounds interesting or different. Something that seems silly might just turn out to be fascinating. My students have researched words for cookies, bread, drinks, ways to go fishing, kinds of cattle, and more.

Once you have each identified a semantic domain to focus on, then each of you will need to ask the other to describe something about the domain (for example, how he bakes bread, what kinds of drinks she likes best). Most likely whoever is doing the describing will begin using words from the semantic domain in question. Whoever is doing the listening should begin writing these down to form a collection of words for the analysis.

Next start grouping your collection of words into a **taxonomy.** A taxonomy is a model that shows how words are related to one another by inclusion, or by how they are kinds of something else; it usually has several levels. Delicious and Granny Smith are kinds of apples, apples and pears are kinds of fruit, fruits and vegetables are kinds of produce (or perhaps kinds of things that grow on plants). Lime green and forest green are kinds of green, green and blue are kinds of "cool" colors, "cool" colors are kinds of colors (in general, and in contrast to "warm" colors).

Build your taxonomy by searching for more words that might fit into it. *Ascending* and *descending questions* are the best way to do this. Ascending questions include, Is an *x* a kind of something else? Descending questions include, What other kinds of *x* are there? Remember to use your friend's words and categories as much as possible, not yours. Semantic taxonomies are occasionally referred to as folk taxonomies, suggesting that they are not "scientific" taxonomies that have been developed by biologists or color scientists. But in fact all taxonomies are both *folk* (in the sense that they belong to a specific culture) and *scientific*, in the sense that science is a kind of categorization process. Important taxonomies in the anthropological literature include kinship terminology, color terminology, and sets of words for plants and diseases.

Your taxonomy should have several levels of words. At the top should be a word designating the name of the semantic domain ('produce,' for example). Descending from that word should be a set of other words naming things included in the domain ('fruits' and 'vegetables,' for example). A word that has other words descending from it is called a *node.* The 'fruits' node might have words such as 'apples,' 'pears,' 'peaches,' and so on descending from it. The 'apples' node could include 'Delicious' and 'Granny Smith' or some other set of kinds of apples.

A taxonomy only tells you how the words in a domain are connected. It does not tell you how words are distinguished from one another. For this you will need to do a **componential analysis** (also called a **feature analysis** or a **contrast analysis**). Componential analysis reveals the important components (or features, or contrasts) of a meaning system. Any set of words under a node in your taxonomy are fair game for a componential analysis. They will share at least one **semantic** feature (or component, or characteristic) that distinguishes them from words in other nodes. Delicious and Granny Smith share the feature or characteristic of being apples and not any other kind of fruit. Apples and pears share the features or characteristics that make them fruit and not vegetables. But if I send you to the market to buy Granny Smith apples, you will need to know how to recognize them if there are no printed labels there. The feature of greenness should help here, or perhaps the feature of roundness, as Granny Smith apples have both of these characteristics and Delicious apples do not. Asking **contrast questions** (How are x and y different from z? How are y and z different from x?) will help you to discover the semantic features (components, contrasts) that your friend uses to separate the words (and categories of words) in his or her taxonomy.

The words and their distinctive features should be presented in the form of a chart. On a separate sheet of paper, arrange the set of words in a node along the left side of the chart. List the features that are useful in distinguishing the different words from one another along the top of the chart. Indicate, in each cell of the chart, whether the feature is present or absent for the word in question. Here are two different ways to present the analysis:

Kind of Apple	Feature: Color	Feature: Shape
Granny Smith	green	round
Delicious	red	not round

Kind of Apple	Feature: Greenness	Feature: Roundness
Granny Smith	yes	yes
Delicious	no	no

With a collection of words and a taxonomy and contrast analysis in hand, you will have successfully learned something of your friend's worldview, or mental map, and have developed a model that will help you to use the words in that semantic domain as your friend does, with the same range of meanings and distinctions. Try it. It's fun and you will learn a lot. If your friend is from another culture, you may find yourself learning a new language as well.

WEB EXERCISES

2.1   Consult the standardized color chart that is included on the inside front cover of this book (or follow the appropriate link on the companion website). Use that chart to identify the colors for which you have basic color terms. Find the focal point on the chart for each of your basic color terms. Which is the bluest blue, for example, or the reddest red? Using the blank charts provided in Figure 2.1 in this workbook, mark each focal point with an "x." Then note the boundaries of each term. How far does blue extend out from the focal point, for example? How far does red extend out? Don't worry if some areas of the chart are not named or included in the boundaries that you draw. Next, ask a friend to go through the same exercise using a blank chart. Finally, using a third chart, draw lines and place marks to indicate the similarities and differences in color terms, foci, and boundaries between the languages. Use an "x" for your focal points and a "y" for your friend's focal points to help distinguish them. Comment on the differences and similarities between your two charts. Do you both speak the same language? If so, what accounts for any differences that you find?

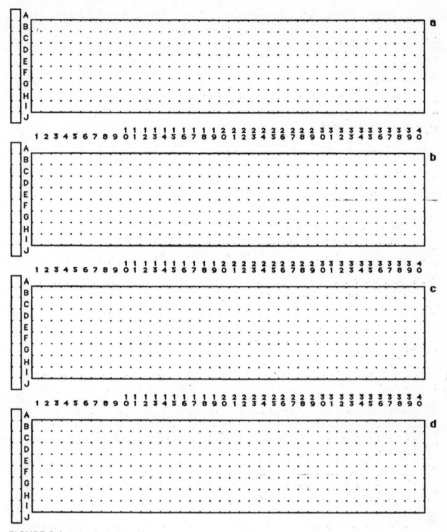

FIGURE 2.1 Blank Color Charts

Courtesy of Rob MacLaury; used by permission.

2.2   Follow the links on the companion website to the dictionaries of Inuit. Explore the dictionary listings and compare the range and variety of words in Inuit with the range and variety of words in your own language for an area that interests you. What similarities and differences do you see in the ways that the two languages reflect cultural emphases?

2.3   Search the InfoTrac database for articles about language and culture.

2.4   Search the InfoTrac database for articles about Sapir and Whorf and their influence on linguistic anthropology.

GUIDED PROJECTS

Language Creating

Think about what you would like to have as an important focus for your language. Discuss some possibilities with your group (weather, plants, animals, foods, drinks, health, diseases, schoolwork, parties, transportation, etc.). Be prepared to remember what you have chosen so that you can use it as a cultural emphasis when it comes time to create actual words for your language. Give your instructor two copies of a brief report listing your group name, the names of the individuals present who contributed to today's work, and the cultural focus you have selected.

Conversation Partnering

2.1   Compare basic color terms with your conversation partner. Follow the instructions given for Web Exercise 2.1 using the color charts and blanks provided. Discuss some of the possible ways that you and your conversation partner might miscommunicate in describing the colors of specific items.

2.2   Compare kinship terms with your conversation partner. Use the two kinship diagrams provided in Figure 2.2 to do this. The conventions on the kinship diagram are standard anthropological ones: circles are females, triangles are males, the square is *ego* (or you, as a point of reference), the = sign means marriage, the vertical bars indicate descent (parent to child, for example), and the horizontal bars indicate siblings (brothers and sisters).

Write the kin terms that you use in *your language* onto one of the diagrams. Be sure that you include terms for all three generations shown in the chart: grandparents, parents/aunts/uncles, and yourself/brothers/sisters/cousins. *Be sure that you only use kin terms and not actual names of family members.* You are *not* creating a genealogical chart! You are creating a chart of the *words* people use to refer to their relatives ("aunt," not "Aunt Pearl," for example). Also be sure you are using kin *terms* and not phrases which describe the relationships (use "aunt," for example, and not "mother's sister," or "father's sister"). Do not add more symbols to the chart unless there is a kin term used in your language for the position designated; if you have different terms for older and younger brother, for example, you may need to add special symbols to the chart.

After you have filled in your kin terms, show the two diagrams to your conversation partner. Ask him/her to help you fill in the other diagram with the terms that *his/her language* uses for the same three generations of kin types. *Make it clear to your conversation partner that you are only asking about kin terms, and not the names of actual family members.* Your conversation partner may be nervous about this until you have made it clear. Note that it may be impolite to ask about actual family members in some cultures. Be sensitive to this possibility and do not pry. As with the diagram for your own language, expand to include additional symbols if the kin term system seems to require it. *Do not* include your conversation partner's actual name anywhere on the page.

Finally, using the space beneath the two diagrams, write a short essay discussing the similarities and differences between the two kinship term systems that you have collected. Discuss what the differences might imply in terms of cultural emphasis in your two cultures. Discuss what adjustments in worldview each of you would have to make in order to communicate effectively about specific kinship relations. *Remember that you must not include your conversation partner's name anywhere in your essay or on your kinship charts.*

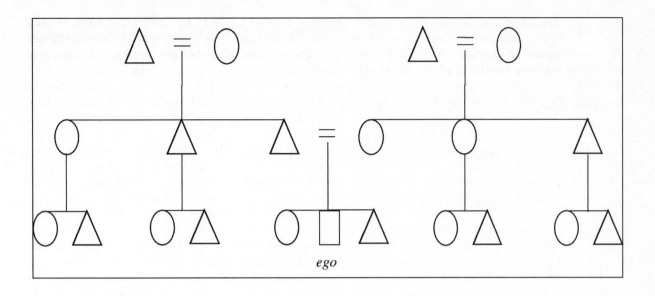

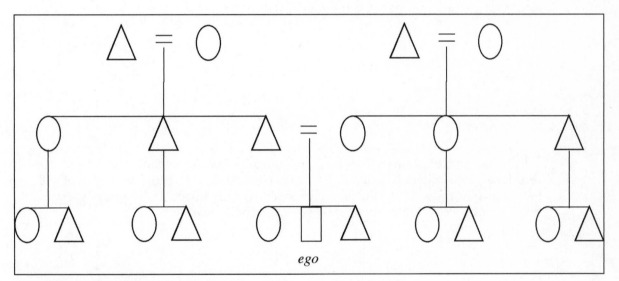

FIGURE 2.2 Kinship Diagrams

Courtesy of Martin Ottenheimer; used by permission.

2.3   If you already know your conversation partner well, then you may try this exercise. Explore a specific semantic domain in your conversation partner's language. Follow the instructions given in the exercises section. Develop a taxonomy of the semantic domain and a componential analysis showing the contrasts within an individual node in the taxonomy.

2.4   If your conversation partner is having difficulty with a particular semantic domain in your language, see if you can develop a taxonomy and componential analysis that will help to explain how the words in the domain appear to be organized. If the analysis seems helpful to your conversation partner, see if you can explain why.

CHAPTER 3

Sounds

Note: Your instructor will indicate which readings, exercises, and/or projects you should do.

❇ READING

3.0   Phonetic Charting: Consonants and Vowels

To understand the principles by which language sounds are produced, you need to learn how to find your way around phonetic charts for consonants and vowels. This workbook section provides the basic tools for working with consonant and vowel charts. After you get the basics of sound production and charting, we will move on to working with how the sounds are arranged in actual languages.

The best way to get oriented in a consonant chart is to imagine that it is a head, facing left. A drawing of a *sagittal section,* or a *cross section view of a head,* should help to make this clearer. Look at the sagittal section drawing in Figure 3.1, with the places of articulation labeled. Notice that the lips, furthest to the left on the drawing, are also furthest to the left in a consonant chart. Also notice, when comparing the sagittal section with the phonetic chart, that the names of the places of articulation are not always exactly the same as the names of the sounds modified in those places. The glottis, for example, is where glottal (not glottis) sounds are made. Most phonetic charts use the names of the sounds modified rather than the names of the exact places, and we will follow that convention as well.

Consonants According to Place of Articulation
As you read through the description of places in which consonants are formed, refer to the drawing of the sagittal section to locate each place anatomically, and then refer to the phonetic charts for consonants to see how each chart names and locates the different kinds of consonants. In the examples below, the International Phonetic Alphabet is used.
   Glottal: The **glottis** is the space between the vocal cords. Sounds modified here are called **glottal** sounds. You can constrict the glottis just enough to produce the kind of friction that begins the English word *happy.* Or you can close the glottis completely, stopping the air and then releasing it again, producing a glottal stop [ʔ], the kind of sound you hear at the beginning of each syllable in the English word *uh-oh.*
   Pharyngeal: The area above the glottis is called the **pharynx.** Constricting the pharynx enough to produce audible friction creates a **pharyngeal** sound. The Arabic sound called *ain* (written <ع> in Arabic script, written [ʕ] in phonetic symbols) is a pharyngeal sound.
   Uvular sounds are produced by bringing the back of the tongue up to the **uvula,** the soft bit of flesh hanging down at the back of the mouth. The French trilled sound [ʀ], in *rue* 'street' is a uvular sound. So is the Arabic [q].
   Velar: The **velum** is the soft part of the roof of the mouth, just in front of the uvula. In **velar** sounds the back of the tongue meets the velum. English speakers will recognize the

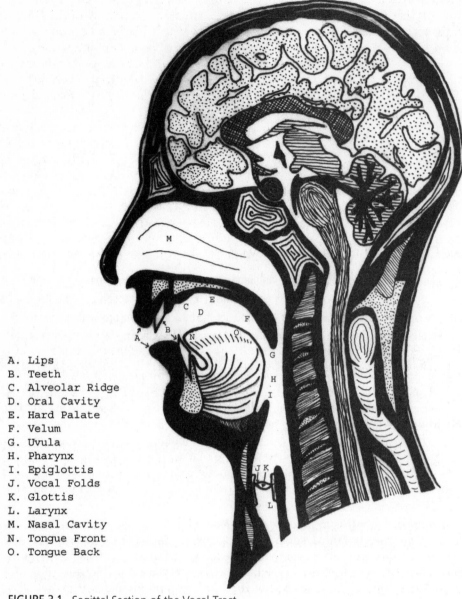

A. Lips
B. Teeth
C. Alveolar Ridge
D. Oral Cavity
E. Hard Palate
F. Velum
G. Uvula
H. Pharynx
I. Epiglottis
J. Vocal Folds
K. Glottis
L. Larynx
M. Nasal Cavity
N. Tongue Front
O. Tongue Back

FIGURE 3.1 Sagittal Section of the Vocal Tract

Courtesy of Alan Joseph; used by permission.

sounds that begin the English words *kill* and *gill* as velar. The [ŋ] sound represented by the
<ng> at the end of the English word *sing* and at the beginning of the Shinzwani word
ngoma 'drum' is also a velar sound.

Palatal: The hard palate refers to the hard part of the roof of the mouth. **Palatal**
sounds are made with the middle part of the tongue and the hard palate. The first sound
of the English word *yellow* is a palatal sound.

Retroflex: Your hard palate is also used for **retroflex** sounds. You make these sounds
by bending the tip of your tongue up and back (you could say you are retro-flexing, or back-
bending, your tongue) and bringing it up to (or even just close to) your hard palate. Many

languages, including Shinzwani and Hindi, use retroflex sounds. A retroflex [ʈ] sounds a tiny bit like the sound represented by the <tr> at the beginning of the English word *train*. In American English, in particular, the <r> in words like *bread* or *roof* is a retroflex [ɻ] (although there is some debate about whether it is a consonant or a vowel).

   Alveopalatal (also called **postalveolar** or **palatal-alveolar**) sounds are produced close to the front of the hard palate, right behind the little ridge that is behind your upper teeth. The <sh> and <ch> of the English words *ship* and *chip* are alveopalatal sounds, as is the <cz> of the Czech word *czech*.

   Alveolar: The small ridge just behind your upper front teeth is called the **alveolar ridge.** Sounds produced by the tongue tip at (or a bit in front of) the alveolar ridge are called **alveolar** sounds. Many languages use this area to produce [t, s, r,] and [n]. The kind of <r> sound [ɾ] used in the Spanish word *pero* 'but' is an alveopalatal sound. So is the kind of <r> sound [r] in the Spanish word *perro* 'dog.' Some Americans pronounce their <r> sound as an alveolar [ɹ] rather than as a retroflex.

   Interdental: Often also called **dental,** these sounds are made with the tip of the tongue between the front teeth. The <th> sound in the English word *think* is an **interdental** (or **dental**) sound. So is the <th> sound in the English word *there*. The first of these is voiceless [θ], the second voiced [ð]. Note that some charts make a distinction between dental and interdental, reserving the word "interdental" for sounds where the tongue is between the teeth and using the word "dental" for sounds where the tongue just touches the back of the teeth.

   Labiodental sounds are made with the lower lip against the upper front teeth. The [f] in the English word *first* is labiodental. The [v] in the English word *very* is also labiodental.

   Bilabial sounds are made by putting the two lips together. The [b] in the English word *bill* and the [p] in the English word *pill* are bilabial sounds. Many languages make use of a bilabial [m] sound.

Consonants According to Manner of Articulation

Stops: Sounds in which the air stream is completely stopped, and then released, are called **stops** (or **plosives,** or **ejectives**). As we have mentioned, [p] and [b] are stops. Other common stops are [t, d, k], and [g]. The sound that begins the two syllables of the English word *uh-oh* is called a **glottal stop,** because the air is stopped completely at the point of the glottis, and then released.

   Fricatives: When the air stream is forced to pass through such a narrow space that it develops audible friction, the sound that is made is called a **fricative.** The air may hiss (for voiceless sounds) or buzz (for voiced sounds). Bringing your tongue tip close to the alveolar ridge (behind your upper teeth) to constrain the air passing through will produce the [s] in the English word *sip* (voiceless) or the [z] in the English word *zip* (voiced). Fricatives are sometimes classified as **lateral** or **central,** depending on whether the air passes over the side or the center of the tongue. An example of a lateral fricative is the [ɬ] sound that is spelled with an <l> in Native American languages such as *Tlingit* and *Kwakiutl*. Central fricatives are categorized as **flat** or **grooved,** depending on the shape of the space through which the air passes. For the <th> sound [θ] of English *think,* the space (and the tongue as well) is fairly flat. For the [s] of the English word *soap,* the space is somewhat grooved.

   Affricates: An **affricate** is a combination of a stop plus a fricative. Usually the stop comes first, and when it is released, it is released as a fricative. The <ts> in the English word *cats* is an affricate consisting of a voiceless alveolar stop [t] and a voiceless alveolar fricative [s]. Both sounds do not need to have the same place of articulation, however. An example would be the <x> at the end of the English word *box,* in which a voiceless velar stop [k] combines with the voiceless alveolar fricative [s]. Kenneth Pike's phonetic chart, which will be discussed in detail shortly, gives affricates a separate row of their own, labeling them "affricated stops." The IPA does not give any space at all to affricates on its chart; instead it notes, at the bottom of the page under "other symbols," that "affricates and double articulations can be represented by two symbols joined by a tie bar if necessary." It is interesting to see such different approaches to the same sort of sound. By the way, Pike's chart, with its focus on detail, also provides space for "aspirated stops" and "laterally released stops." Aspirated stops include the [pʰ] that we discussed in the textbook as the sound that is used at the beginnings of English words but not in the middles. Laterally released stops sound like the <tl> part of the English word *bottle* (note that in this case the <e> is not pronounced at all).

Taps/flaps & trills: Not quite a complete stop, **taps** or **flaps** involve a single, quick, tapping motion. The <r> sound of most languages (but not of U.S. English) is a tap. Most U.S. English speakers use a tap to produce the <tt> in the middle of words like *bitter, butter,* and *batter.* (As you can see, spelling and phonetics are definitely not the same thing!) A series of rapid taps produces a **trill.** The French <r> [ʀ] is a voiced uvular trill. Spanish contains two kinds of <r> sounds: one is a tap [ɾ], and the other is a trill [r].

Approximants: These include sounds that English spells as <l>, <r>, <y>, and <w>, in which the articulators create some obstruction to the air flow but not enough to produce friction of any sort. Different charts group and label them differently. Approximants seem to present special challenges in this regard. Take, for example, the sound represented by the English letter <w>. This sound is produced with simultaneous constriction in two parts of your mouth: lips and velar area. You could call it a voiced labial-velar approximant, but where would you put it on a phonetic chart? in the bilabial column, the velar column, or both columns? The IPA notes, at the bottom of the page, that [w] is a voiced labial-velar approximant, while Pike considers it a semi-vowel [w]. Pike treats <y> as a semi-vowel [y], while the IPA considers it a palatal approximant, listing it on the consonant chart as [j]. The <r> of U.S. English is an alveolar approximant [ɹ] (or a retroflex [ɻ] in some dialects) on the IPA chart, but a mid central vowel [r] with a small dot underneath on Pike's chart. Other sound charts may group the [l] and [ɹ] sounds together as liquids, or the [y] (or [j]) and [w] together as glides. Remember that the primary goal of phonetics, and of a phonetic chart, is to describe *how* a sound is produced. Different scholars have tried different approaches to this task over the years, resulting in different charts with different labels. The most important thing is to check and see how the chart you are using describes and labels sounds and then to either use that chart or "translate" the terms and symbols into the system that works best for you (and for the language you are interested in).

Nasals: Recall the velum at the back of your hard palate. The velum can be raised and lowered. If you are breathing through your nose, the velum is lowered. When you articulate sounds like [p], [t], and [k], your velum is raised until it touches the back of the throat (pharynx), forcing the air to exit exclusively through your mouth. If you lower your velum and allow the air to exit through your nose, the sounds produced are called nasals. They include sounds like the [m] in the English word *mother* or the [n] in the English word *next,* or the <ng> [ŋ] in the Shinzwani word *ngoma.* Technically all of these nasals are kinds of stops, since the air is stopped somewhere in the mouth as well as being allowed to escape through the nose.

Phonetic Charts for Consonants

There are two phonetic charts for consonants provided in this workbook: the International Phonetic Alphabet (IPA), shown in Figure 3.2, and Kenneth Pike's, shown in Figure 3.3. You should be familiar with both if you plan to work with languages. As discussed in the textbook, the IPA is becoming more commonly used; but many anthropologists continue to use Pike's symbols and terminology, and some use a combination. Your instructor will decide which chart (and which symbols and terms) you should be using for class projects.

What we call a specific sound (or combination of sounds) and where we place it on a phonetic chart is based on three things: whether it is voiced or voiceless, where it is pro-

THE INTERNATIONAL PHONETIC ALPHABET (revised to 1993, updated 1996)

CONSONANTS (PULMONIC)

	Bilabial	Labiodental	Dental	Alveolar	Postalveolar	Retroflex	Palatal	Velar	Uvular	Pharyngeal	Glottal
Plosive	p b			t d		ʈ ɖ	c ɟ	k g	q ɢ		ʔ
Nasal	m	ɱ		n		ɳ	ɲ	ŋ	N		
Trill	ʙ			r					ʀ		
Tap or Flap				ɾ		ɽ					
Fricative	ɸ β	f v	θ ð	s z	ʃ ʒ	ʂ ʐ	ç ʝ	x ɣ	χ ʁ	ħ ʕ	h ɦ
Lateral fricative				ɬ ɮ							
Approximant		ʋ		ɹ		ɻ	j	ɰ			
Lateral approximant				l		ɭ	ʎ	L			

Where symbols appear in pairs, the one to the right represents a voiced consonant. Shaded areas denote articulations judged impossible.

CONSONANTS (NON-PULMONIC)

Clicks		Voiced implosives		Ejectives	
ʘ	Bilabial	ɓ	Bilabial	'	Examples:
ǀ	Dental	ɗ	Dental/alveolar	p'	Bilabial
ǃ	(Post)alveolar	ʄ	Palatal	t'	Dental/alveolar
ǂ	Palatoalveolar	ɠ	Velar	k'	Velar
ǁ	Alveolar lateral	ʛ	Uvular	s'	Alveolar fricative

VOWELS

Where symbols appear in pairs, the one to the right represents a rounded vowel.

OTHER SYMBOLS

ʍ	Voiceless labial-velar fricative
w	Voiced labial-velar approximant
ɥ	Voiced labial-palatal approximant
ʜ	Voiceless epiglottal fricative
ʢ	Voiced epiglottal fricative
ʡ	Epiglottal plosive

ɕ ʑ Alveolo-palatal fricatives

ɺ Alveolar lateral flap

ɧ Simultaneous ʃ and x

Affricates and double articulations can be represented by two symbols joined by a tie bar if necessary.   k͡p t͡s

SUPRASEGMENTALS

ˈ	Primary stress
ˌ	Secondary stress
	ˌfoʊnəˈtɪʃən
ː	Long eː
ˑ	Half-long eˑ
˘	Extra-short ĕ
ǀ	Minor (foot) group
‖	Major (intonation) group
.	Syllable break ɹi.ækt
‿	Linking (absence of a break)

DIACRITICS

Diacritics may be placed above a symbol with a descender, e.g. ŋ̊

̥	Voiceless	n̥ d̥	̤	Breathy voiced	b̤ a̤	̪	Dental	t̪ d̪
̬	Voiced	s̬ t̬	̰	Creaky voiced	b̰ a̰	̺	Apical	t̺ d̺
ʰ	Aspirated	tʰ dʰ	̼	Linguolabial	t̼ d̼	̻	Laminal	t̻ d̻
̹	More rounded	ɔ̹	ʷ	Labialized	tʷ dʷ	̃	Nasalized	ẽ
̜	Less rounded	ɔ̜	ʲ	Palatalized	tʲ dʲ	ⁿ	Nasal release	dⁿ
̟	Advanced	u̟	ˠ	Velarized	tˠ dˠ	ˡ	Lateral release	dˡ
̠	Retracted	e̠	ˤ	Pharyngealized	tˤ dˤ	̚	No audible release	d̚
̈	Centralized	ë	̴	Velarized or pharyngealized	ɫ			
̽	Mid-centralized	e̽	̝	Raised	e̝ (ɹ̝ = voiced alveolar fricative)			
̩	Syllabic	n̩	̞	Lowered	e̞ (β̞ = voiced bilabial approximant)			
̯	Non-syllabic	e̯	̘	Advanced Tongue Root	e̘			
˞	Rhoticity	ɚ a˞	̙	Retracted Tongue Root	e̙			

TONES AND WORD ACCENTS

LEVEL			CONTOUR		
e̋ or ˥	Extra high		ě or ˩˥	Rising	
é ˦	High		ê ˥˩	Falling	
ē ˧	Mid		e᷄ ˦˥	High rising	
è ˨	Low		e᷅ ˩˨	Low rising	
ȅ ˩	Extra low		e᷈ ˧˦˧	Rising-falling	
↓	Downstep		↗	Global rise	
↑	Upstep		↘	Global fall	

FIGURE 3.2   International Phonetic Alphabet

Courtesy of the International Phonetic Association.

Chart 2. Symbols for Nonsyllabic Nonvocoids with Egressive Lung Air

General Type of Nonvocoid		Bilabial	Labio-Dental	Inter-Dental	Alveolar	Retro-flex	Alveo-Palatal	Retro-flex	Palatal	Velar	Back Velar	Uvular	Phar-yngeal	Glottal
Stops														
One-segment Unaspirated	vl.	p		t̪	t	ṭ			k̟	k	k̟ (q)		ḳ̇	ʔ
	vd.	b		d̪	d	ḍ			ɡ̟	g	ɡ̣ (G)			
Two-segment Aspirated	vl.	pʰ (pˤ)[1]			tʰ (tˤ)					kʰ (kˤ)				
	vd.	bʱ (bˤ)			dʱ (dˤ)					ɡʱ (ɡˤ)				
Affricated	vl.	pɸ		tθ	ts (c)		tʃ (č)			kx				
	vd.	bβ		dð	dz (ʒ)		dʒ (ǰ)			ɡɣ				
Laterally released	vl.				tɬ (ƛ)									
	vd.				dl (λ)									
Fricatives														
Central Flat	vl.	ɸ	f	θ	θ̠	ṣ		x̌		x	x̣			
	vd.	β	v	ð	ð̠	ẓ		ǰ		ɣ	ɣ̣			
Grooved	vl.	ƕ̥+[2]			s	ʃ̣	š							
	vd.	ƕ+			z	ẓ	ž							
Lateral	vl.				ɬ+									
	vd.				ɬ+									
Frictionless														
Nasal	vl.	m̥ (M)			n̥ (N)	ṇ̥	ɲ̥ (Ñ)			ŋ̥ (N)				
	vd.	m			n	ṇ	ɲ			ŋ				
Lateral	vl.				l̥ (L)	l̥̇	l̥ʸ							
	vd.				l	l̇	lʸ							
Vibrants														
Flapped	vl.				ɾ̥							ɾ̥̇		
	vd.				ɾ									
Trilled	vl.	ʙ̥			r̥									
	vd.	ʙ			r									

[For h, ḥ, and ẖ, see foot-notes, p. 5]

[1]Parentheses enclose optional symbols.

[2]For [w], [y], [r], and their voiceless counterparts, see p. 5.

FIGURE 3.3 Kenneth Pike's Consonant Chart

Source: K. L. Pike, Phonemics: A Technique for Reducing Languages to Writing (Ann Arbor: University of Michigan Press). Copyright © 1947 University of Michigan Press. Reprinted by permission.

Chart 1. Symbols for Voiced Syllabic Vocoids						
		Front		**Central**		**Back**	
		Unrounded	Rounded	Unrounded	Rounded	Unrounded	Rounded
High	close	ɨ	ü	ɨ	ʉ	ï	u
	open	ɩ	ü̇			ï̈	ʊ
Mid	close	e	ö	ə ɚ²		ë	o
	open	ɛ		ʌ			
Low	close	æ	ɔ̈				ɔ
	open	a		ɑ			ʋ

Note: Footnote 2 says, "With retroflexed or retracted tongue formation."

FIGURE 3.4 Kenneth Pike's Vowel Chart

Source: K. L. Pike, Phonemics: A Technique for Reducing Languages to Writing (Ann Arbor: University of Michigan Press). Copyright © 1947 University of Michigan Press. Reprinted by permission.

duced, and how it is produced. For example, the [p] in the English word *spill* is a voiceless bilabial stop. It should appear in the bilabial column of a phonetic chart, in the row labeled "stops." Different charts align voiced and voiceless sounds differently. Some (such as the IPA) put voiced sounds to the right of their voiceless "equivalents." Some (such as Kenneth Pike's) put voiced sounds underneath their voiceless "equivalents." The [b] in the English word ***bill*** is a voiced bilabial stop and should appear close to the [p] on a phonetic chart, either to its right or just below it. The difference in charts can be confusing, but it need not be. Just pay attention to the labels each one uses and follow the columns and rows accordingly. Many students find that creating and memorizing a mental picture lining up the three voiceless stops [p], [t], and [k] from left to right and treating them as "primary sounds" (something like primary colors perhaps, but using the names "bilabial," "alveolar," and "velar" rather than "red," "blue," and "yellow") helps them to find their way around any phonetic chart.

Phonetic Charts for Vowels
The IPA includes a chart for vowels on its one-page chart. This workbook also includes Kenneth Pike's chart for vowels (Fig. 3.4). Although Pike's chart is presented as a rectangle, the way that the tongue moves back in the mouth as it gets lower suggests that the IPA chart is a somewhat more graphic representation of the arrangement of vowels in the mouth. Close observers will notice that Pike's front-unrounded vowels follow this tongue movement slightly. As you explore the differences between the two charts, be sure to notice that the IPA and Pike use slightly different words for describing tongue height and mouth openness.

◈ WRITING/DISCUSSION EXERCISES

3.1   Use the drawing of the sagittal section to work your way through the different phonetic charts. The more you understand about how sounds are produced, the easier it will be to play with them and learn to pronounce them yourself.

3.2   Locate each place of articulation on the drawing of the sagittal section. Then locate the relevant column in one (or both) of the phonetic charts. Practice pronouncing sounds in each place of articulation. Which of those sounds are in the language(s) that you speak?

3.3 Read through the section on consonants according to manner of articulation. Then locate the relevant row in one (or both) of the phonetic charts. Practice pronouncing sounds according to each manner of articulation. Which of those sounds are in the language(s) that you speak?

3.4 Notice that Pike's chart includes a row for affricates and that the IPA chart does not. How are affricates written using the IPA system? Give some examples of affricates written according to each notational system. Discuss the difference between the ways in which the two charts represent affricates. Which approach seems more logical to you? Why?

3.5   Create a phonetic chart for the language(s) that you speak.

3.6   Compare the two vowel charts (IPA and Pike). Comment on the difference in labels for tongue height and mouth openness. Notice that some symbols are used by both charts but appear in slightly different locations. Do you think this means that the symbols in the two different charts represent different vowels? or that they represent the same vowel, but the charts disagree about where in the mouth that vowel is pronounced?

3.7 Develop a list of references (books, journal articles, magazine articles, websites) where you can find more information about phonology.

3.8 Describe one way in which an understanding of phonology might contribute to your own major field of study.

◈ PRACTICE WITH LANGUAGES

3.1 Charting Consonants: New Zealand

A school in New Zealand had pupils from many Pacific Islands. One day a teacher gave each of four pupils a piece of candy.

The Maori child said	[fæŋk yu]
The Luangiuan child said	[sæŋk yu]
The Rarotongan child said	[tæŋk yu]
The American child said	[gat ɛniy mɔr]

Which of the consonant inventories below is Maori? Which is Luangiuan? Which is Rarotongan? (Refer to the IPA consonant chart for guidance.)

```
p     k  ʔ          p   t   k          p   t   k   ʔ
 m       ŋ           m  n  ŋ            m  n  ŋ
  v  s     h          f       h          v
      l               w   r                  r
```

Explain, in *phonetic* terms, why you made the choices that you made for the charts.

Use the *sound charts* to explain why the Maori, Luangiuan, and Rarotongan children did not say [θæŋk yu].

Use the *sound charts* to explain why the Maori child said [fæŋk yu] and not [tæŋk yu].

3.2 Minimal Pairs and Phonemic Distinctiveness

As we discussed in the textbook, the concept of minimal pairs applies in any language. Once you have charted the phones of a language and have identified suspicious pairs, you should be able to gather sufficient data to determine whether similar sounds are distinct phonemes or not. The following exercises will give you some practice with minimal pairs in Western and non-Western languages. Each exercise highlights a pair of sounds that, on the phonetic chart, appears to be "suspicious" and gives you lists of words, arranged into columns, that use one or more of the two sounds in question. Find and mark the minimal pairs in each exercise. Note: Words that are marked with an asterisk (*) contain both sounds.

3.2a Shinzwani (Comoro Islands)

words with [t]		words with [ṭ]	
1 tuku	a small shop	5 nṭa	stingray
2 ʃito	a gem	6 ʃinṭu	something
3 nta	wax	7 ṭove	dirt
4 mataba	manioc leaves	8 maṭa	oil

3.2b Hindi

words with [kʰ]		words with [k]	
1 kʰa	eat	5 kal	death/time
2 kʰəl	evil person	6 kʊl	total
3 kʰal	skin	7 kəl	tomorrow/yesterday
4 kʰʊl	(to) open	8 ka	of

3.2c Czech
Long vowels are marked with [ː]

words with [r]		words with [ř]	
1 riziko	risk, hazard	7 hɔřkiː	bitter
2 trh	market	8 řiːzɛk	slice, cutlet
3 vrabɛts	sparrow	9 břiːza	birch
4 hɔrkiː	hot	10 vřɛd	ulcer
5 briːza	warm sea breeze	11 třɛsk	a clinking noise
6 trɛska	codfish	12 tři	three

3.2d French

words with [e]		words with [ɛ]	
1 epin	thorn	5 ɛsprit	spirit
2 etwal	star	6 ɛskargo	snail
3 te	tea	7 sɛl	salt
4 tele	television	8 tɛ	pillow case

3.2e Chatino (Mexico)
Note: The numbers indicate relative pitches. [³] is a higher tone than [²]. The small circles under the vowels indicate voicelessness. [ʔ] is a glottal stop.

words with [³]		words with [²]	
1 ta̯ʔˀa³	sibling	4 tu̥ʔwˀa²	mouth
2 ki̥tˀa³	you will wait	5 ta̯ʔˀa²	fiesta
3 tu̥ʔwˀa³	forty	6 si̥ʔi²	is not

3.3 Phonemes and Allophones

As described in the textbook, *allophones* are variations in the pronunciation of a single phoneme in a language. Allophones are generally heard as a single sound (or as minor and insignificant variants of a single sound) by the speakers of the language in question. Remember that allophones generally "complement" one another by occurring in different phonetic environments. This arrangement is referred to as complementary distribution or conditioned variation.

An example of a phoneme with allophones is the English /t/. This phoneme has three different allophones in English: [tʰ] (aspirated), [t] (not aspirated), and [tˀ] (not audibly released). Each occurs in a distinct phonetic environment, as follows:

words with [tʰ]		words with [t]		words with [tˀ]	
1 [tʰɪk]	tick	4 [stɪk]	stick	7 [sɪtˀ]	sit
2 [tʰæn]	tan	5 [stænd]	stand	8 [kætˀ]	cat
3 [tʰon]	tone	6 [ston]	stone	9 [kotˀ]	coat

There are two ways in which this can be written up:

1. as a descriptive statement:
   /t/ has allophones [tʰ, t, and t̚]
   [tʰ] in word-initial position
   [t] following [s]
   [t̚] in word-final position

2. as a rule:
   /t/

   → [tʰ] #___V
   → [t] [s]___V
   → [t̚] V___#

represents the silence at the beginning or end of a word, V represents any vowel, and [s] represents a specific sound (voiceless alveolar fricative). Although it is not used here, note that C can stand for any consonant.

Allophone Conditioning

Note that the overall phonological environment of a word (or even a series of words) conditions the exact way in which different allophones of a phoneme are pronounced. A back vowel, for example, might cause the speakers of a particular language to produce a further-back version of a consonant. A nasal consonant might influence a neighboring vowel to be produced with nasalization. When one sound is drawn closer to another in this way, the process is called **assimilation;** one sound is said to have assimilated to another. Assimilation can cause sounds to be raised or lowered, voiced or devoiced, aspirated or unaspirated, and more, depending on the phonological environment and the way in which it "conditions" the sounds around it. Although these slight variations in sound may make no difference to the meanings of the words, they do serve several important linguistic and social functions, allowing speakers of a language to distinguish social and regional dialects as well as perceived "correctness" of accent.

To discover the conditions that cause allophone variation, you need to carefully compare the phonological environments of the allophones in question. Usually there is some feature present in the environment of one of the allophones that is not present in the environment of the other. And usually the two environments are "complementary" in some way: they are distinct from one another and do not overlap. When you can identify the difference between the two environments in phonological terms, then you will have found the conditioning for the variation of the allophones.

The exercises that follow provide practice in identifying the conditioning environments for allophones. You may write up your analyses as descriptive statements or as rules (follow the example provided earlier in this section).

3.3a English

Transcribe the following words into phonetic form and work out the conditioning environments for the phoneme /p/ in English.

words with [pʰ]	words with [p]	words with [p̚]
1 pit	5 spit	9 tip
2 pat	6 spat	10 tap
3 poke	7 spoke	11 cope
4 peek	8 speak	12 reap

Compare the allophones of /p/ with the allophones of /t/ in English. How are the two patterns of distribution similar to one another?

Based on this similarity, make a prediction about the English phoneme /k/. Do you expect it to have three allophones as well? Give examples of English words with /k/ in these three different positions.

3.3b KiSwahili

words with [ɔ]		words with [o]	
1 ŋgɔma	drum	9 ndoto	dream
2 ɲɔmbe	cattle	10 ndogo	little
3 ɔmba	pray	11 mboga	vegetable
4 ɔna	see	12 okota	pick up
5 ɔŋgeza	increase	13 modʒa	one
6 ɲɔɲa	nurse	14 soka	axe
7 pɔɲa	cure	15 watoto	children
8 ɲɔŋga	strangle	16 dʒɔgo	rooster

3.3c German

words with [d]		words with [t]	
1 damə	woman	6 axt	eight
2 abdrʊk	copy	7 fast	almost
3 kɪnder	children	8 kɪnt	child
4 dɛnkɛn	think	9 gɛlt	money
5 gɛldlix	monetary	10 hʊnt	dog

3.3d Korean

words with [l]		words with [r]	
1 tal	moon	6 keːri	distance
2 talda	sweet	7 irure	reaches
3 sul	wine	8 saram	person
4 sosəl	novel	9 puran	unrest
5 kwasil	fruit	10 uri	we

3.3e Japanese

words with [ʃ]

1 ʃimasu   do
2 ʃiroi   white
3 ʃinu   die

words with [s]

4 saka   hill
5 sora   sky
6 sensei   teacher

3.3f English

words with [ķ] (fronted)

1 ķip   keep
2 ķil   keel
3 kɪl   kill
4 ķyur   cure

words with [k]

5 kət   cut
6 kəp   cup
7 kæt   cat
8 kæp   cap

words with [ḵ] (backed)

 9 ḵul   cool
10 ḵuḵi   cookie*
11 ḵʊd   could
12 sḵul   school

3.3g isiZulu

words with [ɔ]

 1 ɓɔna   see
 2 ɓɔpʰa   bind
 3 mɔsa   despoil
 4 umɔna   jealousy
 5 imɔtɔ   car
 6 iǃɔlɔ   small of back
 7 iǁɔllɔ   frog
 8 isiǀɔlɔ   head ring
 9 iɓɔdwe   pot
10 isithɔmbe   picture
11 indɔdara   son
12 umfɔkazi   strange man

words with [o]

13 iɓoni   grasshopper
14 umondli   guardian
15 umosi   one who roasts
16 inoni   fat
17 udoli   doll
18 umǁolli   story teller
19 imomfu   jersey cow
20 lolu   this
21 isitofu   stove
22 nomuthi   and the tree
23 udodile   you acted like a man
24 ibokisi   box

3.3h Totonac (Mexico)

There are three vowel phonemes here: /i/, /a/, and /u/. Describe the pattern for each one. Then describe the distribution for voiced and voiceless vowels in general.

 1 tʃapsḁ   he stacks
 2 tʃilinksḁ   it resounded
 3 kasitti̥   cut it
 4 kuku̥   uncle
 5 ɬkakḁ   peppery
 6 miki̥   snow
 7 snapapḁ   white
 8 stapu̥   beans
 9 ʃumpi̥   porcupine
10 taaqhu̥   you plunged in
11 tihaʃɬi̥   he rested
12 tukʃɬi̥   it broke

3.3i Farsi (Iran)

words with [r]

1 ærtéʃ   army
2 fársí   Persian
3 qædri   a little bit
4 ráh   road
5 rást   right
6 ræng   paint
7 ríʃ   beard
8 rúz   day

words with [ɾ]

 9 aharí   starched
10 bæradæɾ   brother*
11 bérid   go
12 biræng   pale
13 borós   hairbrush
14 tʃéra   why
15 daríd   you have
16 ʃiriní   pastry

words with [ɹ̥]

1	ahaɹ̥	starch
2	axæɹ̥	last
3	ænaɹ̥	pomegranate
4	behtæɹ̥	better
5	tʃáɹ̥	four
6	tʃédʒuɹ̥	what kind?
7	hærtowɹ̥	however*
8	ʃíɹ̥	lion

WEB EXERCISES

3.1   Follow the link on the companion website to the University of Oxford's Phonetics Laboratory page. Once there, use the photos, diagrams, and video clips to get better acquainted with the details of speech production. How does this site help you to understand voicing and voicelessness better?

3.2   Follow the links on the companion website to the UCLA Phonetics Laboratory. Once there, watch the video clips showing how speech sounds are produced. How do these videos enhance your understanding of speech sound production?

3.3 Follow the link on the companion website to the University of Toronto's interactive sagittal section site. Experiment with the site until you understand how sounds are modified in the vocal tract.

3.4 Follow the link on the companion website to the International Phonetics Association. Write a short summary of the history of the association. How and why did its members develop the International Phonetic Alphabet?

3.5 Follow the link on the companion website to the University of Lausanne's online phonetics course. Navigate to the interactive IPA chart and click on the symbols to hear the different sounds. This is an excellent way to practice hearing the sounds and recognizing the symbols for them.

3.6 Follow the link on the companion website to Kenneth Pike's brief autobiography. Discuss how Pike's experiences learning languages in the field contributed to his ideas about etics and emics.

3.7   Follow the link on the companion website to read a description of Ken Pike's famous fifteen-minute monolingual language learning demonstrations. Discuss how you could use your own developing skills in linguistic anthropology to learn a new language in a monolingual situation. Have you ever been in a monolingual situation like the one Pike simulates in his demonstrations? What did you do? How did it work? What would you do differently now that you are learning the basics of linguistic anthropology?

3.8   Follow the link on the companion website to the Language Construction Kit. This is a chatty step-by-step guide to creating "alien" languages. You can learn a lot about linguistics from this site while having fun at the same time.

3.9   Search the InfoTrac database for articles about phonology.

◈ GUIDED PROJECTS

Language Creating

If your instructor has assigned this project, then this is the time to choose the sounds for your new language. Your instructor will be your guide here, providing details as you need them. As you complete each step in the process, hand in two copies of your group's work. Be sure to include your group's name as well as the names of all of the individuals present who contributed to the day's work.

Conversation Partnering

If your instructor has assigned this project, you may be asked to develop a contrastive consonant chart showing the consonant phonemes of your conversation partner's language and your own. Your instructor will provide more details.

CHAPTER 4

Words and Sentences

Note: Your instructor will indicate which readings, exercises, and/or projects you should do.

※ READING

4.0   "Tenses and Time Travel" by Douglas Adams

Douglas Adams's science fiction "trilogy" pokes fun at a great many things, including the concept of trilogy. Although a trilogy should be a series of three books, Adams's *The Hitchhiker's Guide to the Galaxy,* from which this is an excerpt, contains well more than three books. Here, in the second book in the series, he plays with the idea of what time travel might do to the ways in which people use tenses. In the process, he makes up some tenses.

The major problem is quite simply one of grammar, and the main work to consult in this matter is Dr. Dan Streetmentioner's *Time Traveler's Handbook of 1001 Tense Formations.* It will tell you, for instance, how to describe something that was about to happen to you in the past before you avoided it by time-jumping forward two days in order to avoid it. The event will be described differently according to whether you are talking about it from the standpoint of your own natural time, from a time in the further future, or a time in the further past, and is further complicated by the possibility of conducting conversations while you are actually traveling from one time to another with the intention of becoming your own mother or father.

Most readers get as far as the Future Semiconditionally Modified Subinverted Plagal Past Subjunctive Intentional before giving up, and in fact in later editions of the book all the pages beyond this point have been left blank to save on printing costs.

The Hitchhiker's Guide to the Galaxy skips lightly over this tangle of academic abstraction, pausing only to note that the term "Future Perfect" has been abandoned since it was discovered not to be.

WRITING/DISCUSSION EXERCISES

4.1   It has been said that English has only two simple tenses, the present and the past. This is because these are the only two tenses that do not need additional helping verbs for expression. *I eat,* for example, is the simple present tense, and *I ate* is the simple past tense. Future tense, on the other hand, requires an additional helping verb, as in *I **will** eat,* and therefore is seen as a "complex" tense. What impact, if any, do you think this situation has on the way English speakers think about the world? Would you say English speakers find it easier to think about the past than about the future? Discuss this with your classmates, or write a short essay about the difference between simple and complex tenses in English.

4.2   Read through Exercise 4.1 and think about the same question with regard to other languages you have studied. Which of those languages' tenses are "simple" and which are "complex"? Is the list the same as in your language? What do you think the differences, if any, might imply?

4.3   What other languages have you studied? Did any of them have tenses or verb categories that you were not familiar with from your own language? What kinds of difficulties did you encounter in trying to learn how to use those tenses or verb categories that were new to you?

4.4   What other languages have you studied? Did any of them have ways of categorizing nouns that were not familiar to you from your own language (such as case or grammatical gender)? What kinds of difficulties did you encounter in trying to learn how to use those categories?

◈ PRACTICE WITH LANGUAGES

4.1   Kanuri (Nigeria)

1	gana	small	6 nəmgana	smallness
2	kura	big	7 nəmkura	bigness
3	kurugu	long	8 nəmkurugu	length
4	karite	excellent	9 nəmkarite	excellence
5	dibi	bad	10 nəmdibi	badness

a. What kind of affix is shown in entries 6–10 (Kanuri)? What is its form? What is its approximate meaning in English?

b. If the Kanuri word /kədʒi/ is equivalent to the English word 'sweet,' what is the Kanuri word for 'sweetness'?

c. If the Kanuri word /nəmŋəla/ is equivalent to the English word 'goodness,' what is the Kanuri word for 'good'?

4.2   LuGanda (Uganda)

1	omukazi	woman	6 abakazi	women
2	omusawo	doctor	7 abasawo	doctors
3	omusika	heir	8 abasika	heirs
4	omuwala	girl	9 abawala	girls
5	omulenzi	boy	10 abalenzi	boys

a. What type of affixes are shown? What are their forms? What are their approximate meanings in English?

b. If the LuGanda word /abaloŋgo/ is equivalent to the English word 'twins,' what is the LuGanda word for 'twins'?

4.3   Shinzwani (Comoro Islands)

1 nzwani	the island that Europeans call Anjouan
munzwani	a person from the island of nzwani
wanzwani	people from the island of nzwani
shinzwani	the language spoken on the island of nzwani

2 farantsa the country that Europeans call France
 mufarantsa a person from farantsa
 wafarantsa people from farantsa
 shifarantsa the language spoken in farantsa

3 ngereza the country that Europeans call England
 mungereza a person from ngereza
 wangereza people from ngereza
 shingereza the language spoken in ngereza

a. What kind of affixes are being used here?

b. List each affix and give the approximate English meaning for each one.

c. List the Shinzwani root forms for 'Anjouan,' 'France,' and 'England.'

d. What seems to be the relationship between the root form and the three words derived from it?

e. Given /marikan/ 'America,' what is the most likely word for 'American'? What is the most likely word for the language spoken in /marikan/?

f. Given /shintiri/ 'Pig Latin,' is it possible to guess at the root form? What would be the meaning of the root form, if it existed?

4.4 Kurdish

1 aaqil	wise	6 aaqilii	forethought
2 diz	a robber	7 dizii	robbery
3 draiʒi	long	8 draiʒii	length
4 zaanaa	wise	9 zaanaaii	erudition
5 garm	warm	10 garmii	warmth

a. What kind of affix is shown in entries 6–10 (Kurdish)? What is its form? What is its approximate meaning in English?

b. Can you explain why the English word 'wise' is given as the equivalent for both /aaqil/ and /zaanaa/? Can you explain why two *different* English words are given as equivalents for /aaqilii/ and /zaanaaii/? What, in general, seems to be the difference between /aaqil/ and /zaanaa/? Can you suggest better English equivalents for /aaqil/ and /zaanaa/ that will show the contrast between them more clearly?

c. If Kurdish /raas/ means 'true' in English, what is a likely meaning for /raasii/?

4.5   Czech

1	žena	woman	5	ženy	women
2	ženy	woman's	6	žen	women's
3	ženě	to the/a woman	7	ženám	to the women
4	ženou	by the/a woman	8	ženami	by the women

a. What type of affixes are shown? List each one and give its approximate meaning in English.

b. What seems to be the root form for 'woman/women' in Czech?

c. If the Czech word /kočka/ is equivalent to the English word 'cat,' how would you say 'to the cats' in Czech?

4.6   Bontoc (Philippine Islands)

1	fikas	strong	5	fumikas	he is becoming strong
2	kilad	red	6	kumilad	he is becoming red
3	bato	stone	7	bumato	he is becoming stone
4	fusul	enemy	8	fumusul	he is becoming an enemy

a. What type of affix is shown? What is its form? Where is it attached? What is its approximate meaning in English?

b. If the Bontoc word /pusi/ is equivalent to the English word 'poor,' what is the most likely English equivalent for /pumusi/?

c. If the Bontoc word /ŋitad/ is equivalent to the English word 'dark,' what is the most likely Bontoc equivalent for 'he is becoming dark'?

d. If the Bontoc word /pumukaw/ is equivalent to 'he is becoming white' in English, what is the most likely Bontoc equivalent for 'white'?

4.7 Samoan

1	manao	(he) wishes	9	mananao	(they) wish
2	matua	(he) is old	10	matutua	(they) are old
3	malosi	(he) is strong	11	malolosi	(they) are strong
4	punou	(he) bends	12	punonou	(they) bend
5	savali	(he) travels	13	savavali	(they) travel
6	pese	(he) sings	14	pepese	(they) sing
7	laga	(he) weaves	15	lalaga	(they) weave
8	atamaʔi	(he) is wise	16	atamamaʔi	(they) are wise

a. What type of affix is shown in entries 9–16 (Samoan)? What is its form? Where is it attached? What is its approximate meaning in English?

b. Given /galue/ '(he) works,' what would be the most likely form for '(they) work'?

c. Given /alolofa/ '(they) love,' what would be the most likely form for '(he) loves'?

4.8 Hopi

1	tíri	he gives a start	6	tirírita	he is trembling
2	wíwa	he stumbles	7	wiwáwata	he is hobbling along

3	kʷíla	he takes a step forward	8 kʷilálata	he walks forward
4	ʔími	it makes a bang	9 ʔimímita	it is thundering
5	ngáro	his teeth strike something	10 ngarórota	he is chewing on something

a. What type of affix is shown in entries 6–10 (Hopi)? What is its form (there are three things to note here)? What is its approximate meaning in English?

b. Given /róya/ 'it makes a turn,' what would be the most likely form for 'it is rotating'?

c. Given /ripípita/ 'it is sparkling,' what would be the most likely form for 'it flashes'?

4.9   Tepehua (Mexico)

1 laqatam	one	9 laqakaawt'utu	thirteen
2 laqat'uy	two	10 laqap'uʃam	twenty
3 laqat'utu	three	11 laqap'uʃamtam	twenty-one
4 laqat'aat'ii	four	12 laqap'uʃamkaaw	thirty
5 laqakiis	five	13 laqap'uʃamkaawt'uy	thirty-two
6 laqakaaw	ten	14 laqap'uʃamkaawkiis	thirty-five
7 laqakaawtam	eleven	15 laqat'aatiikiisp'uʃam	four hundred
8 laqakaawt'uy	twelve	16 laqakiiskiisp'uʃam	five hundred

Note: The prefix /laqa-/ is used only with certain nouns:

laqatam kawayuh	one horse
laqat'uy ʃanta	two flowers

Other nouns require different prefixes:

aqʃt'uy alnikii	two pieces of paper
aqʃt'utu ʃaapuuh	three pieces of soap
qankaaw k'iw	ten trees
qankiis maka	five fingers

a. List the morphemes for the following numbers (do not include any of the prefixes):

one _____   five _____

two _____   ten _____

three _____   twenty _____

four _____

b. What would you expect for each of the following?

twenty-five _____

thirty-four _____

three hundred _____

c. What can you state about the order of the morphemes? What are the two different orders in this data? What does each order indicate? How does this compare with English?

4.10 KiSwahili Verbs

1	atanipenda	s/he will like me	15	atanipiga	s/he will beat me
2	atakupenda	s/he will like you	16	atakupiga	s/he will beat you
3	atampenda	s/he will like him/her	17	atampiga	s/he will beat him/her
4	atatupenda	s/he will like us	18	ananipiga	s/he is beating me
5	atawapenda	s/he will like them	19	anakupiga	s/he is beating you
6	nitakupenda	I will like you	20	anampiga	s/he is beating him/her
7	nitampenda	I will like him/her	21	amenipiga	s/he has beaten me
8	nitawapenda	I will like them	22	amekupiga	s/he has beaten you
9	utatupenda	you will like us	23	amempiga	s/he has beaten him/her
10	utampenda	you will like him/her	24	alinipiga	s/he beat me
11	tutampenda	we will like him/her	25	alikupiga	s/he beat you
12	watampenda	they will like him/her	26	alimpiga	s/he beat him/her
13	atakusikia	s/he will hear you	27	wametulipa	they have paid us
14	unamsikia	you hear him/her	28	tulikulipa	we paid you

Note: 'You' is always 'you-singular.' The plural form of 'you' is not included here.

a. Give the KiSwahili morphemes associated with each of the following English forms:

Subjects	Objects	Tenses	Stems
_____ I	_____ me	_____ future	_____ like
_____ you	_____ you	_____ present	_____ beat
_____ s/he	_____ him/her	_____ past	_____ pay
_____ we	_____ us	_____ perfect	_____ hear
_____ they	_____ them	(*Hint:* perfect = have/has)	

b. What is the order of morphemes in a KiSwahili verb? How does this compare to the order of these morphemes/words in equivalent English sentences?

c. Give the probable KiSwahili forms for the following English sentences:

I have beaten them. _____

They are beating me. _____

You have heard me. _____

They will hear us. _____

We paid them. _____

S/he has paid me. _____

We liked you. _____

You like us. _____

d. Give the probable English sentences for the following KiSwahili forms:

atanilipa _____

utawapiga _____

walikupenda _____

nimekusikia _____

4.11 KiSwahili Nouns

Stems

					Stems
1	ubao	plank	mbao	planks	_____
2	ubawa	wing	mbawa	wings	_____
3	udevu	hair	ndevu	hairs	_____
4	ugwe	string	ŋgwe	strings	_____
5	uwati	hut pole	mbati	hut poles	_____
6	uwanda	open place	mbanda	open places	_____
7	uwiŋgu	heaven	mbiŋgu	heavens	_____
8	ulimi	tongue	ndimi	tongues	_____
9	upaŋga	sword	pʰaŋga	swords	_____
10	upindi	bow	pʰindi	bows	_____
11	utambi	lamp wick	tʰambi	lamp wicks	_____
12	utepe	stripe	tʰepe	stripes	_____
13	ukuta	wall	kʰuta	walls	_____
14	ukuni	stick	kʰuni	sticks	_____
15	ukucha	fingernail	kʰucha	fingernails	_____
16	ufunguo	key	funguo	keys	_____
17	ufagio	broom	fagio	brooms	_____
18	ufizi	gum	fizi	gums	_____
19	uvumbi	bit of dust	vumbi	dust	_____
20	usiku	night	siku	nights	_____
21	ushanga	bead	ʃanga	beads	_____
22	wakati	season	ɲakati	seasons	_____
23	wavu	net	ɲavu	nets	_____
24	wayo	footprint	ɲayo	footprints	_____
25	wembe	razor	ɲembe	razors	_____
26	wimbo	song	ɲimbo	songs	_____

Note: /pʰ tʰ kʰ/ are single aspirated phonemes.

All of these words belong to a single noun "class" or category in KiSwahili. Note that each word appears to be made up of both a prefix and a stem. For example, "ubao" is composed of the singular prefix /u-/ and the stem /-bao/. Note also that the prefixes change, depending on the sounds in the stems (and, in a few cases, vice versa). Your task is to find, list, and analyze all of the variations in the prefixes and the stems.

a. List all of the stems in the spaces provided above. In some cases you will need to list two different allomorphs for a stem; for example, /-wiŋgu/ and /-biŋgu/ are both stems for word number 7. Since a stem never occurs without an affix in KiSwahili, be sure to write each stem with a hyphen.

b. List all of the prefixes in the following table. For example, list both /u-/ and /w-/ for the singular. Since prefixes never occur without stems in Ki-Swahili, be sure to write each prefix with a hyphen. The singular prefixes have been filled in for you. Complete the chart, giving all of the plural prefix variations.

c. For each prefix, give a list of how the stems used with that prefix begin, and list the item numbers as well. The stems and item numbers for the singular prefixes have been filled in for you. Complete the chart for all of the plural prefix variations.

	Prefixes	Used with stems beginning in:	Items numbered
Singular	/u-/	/b, d, g, w, ... /	1–25
	/w-/	/a, e, ... /	22–26
Plural			

d. Try to make a more general statement about the way in which the plural prefix varies. Consult a phonetic chart for assistance with this task. Note similarities of place or manner between prefixes and the stems they attach to. For example, note the fact that /m-/ in the prefix and /-b/ in the stem in word number 1 are both bilabial and both voiced. See what other phonetic similarities you can find.

e. For those stems that change, describe the changes. Refer to a phonetic chart for terminology to use. Note especially stems numbered 5–8 and stems numbered 9–15. Which form do you think should be considered as the base form from which both singular and plural forms can be derived? Why?

4.12 KiSwahili Noun Classes

					Prefixes	Stems
1	mtoto	child	watoto	children	_____	_____
2	mtu	person	watu	people	_____	_____
3	mpiʃi	cook	wapiʃi	cooks	_____	_____
4	mgeni	stranger	wageni	strangers	_____	_____
5	mswahili	Swahili person	waswahili	Swahili people	_____	_____
6	mʃale	arrow	miʃale	arrows	_____	_____
7	mti	tree	miti	trees	_____	_____
8	mzigo	load	mizigo	loads	_____	_____
9	mkufu	chain	mikufu	chains	_____	_____
10	mtego	trap	mitego	traps	_____	_____
11	ŋgoma	drum	ŋgoma	drums	_____	_____
12	ŋgao	shield	ŋgao	shields	_____	_____
13	ndizi	banana	ndizi	bananas	_____	_____
14	ndoto	dream	ndoto	dreams	_____	_____
15	mboga	vegetable	mboga	vegetables	_____	_____
16	mbu	mosquito	mbu	mosquitos	_____	_____
17	kʰuku	chicken	kʰuku	chickens	_____	_____

				Prefixes	Stems
18	kʰamba	rope	kʰamba	ropes	_____	_____
19	tʰembo	elephant	tʰembo	elephants	_____	_____
20	pʰembe	horn	pʰembe	horns	_____	_____
21	nzige	locust	nzige	locusts	_____	_____
22	safari	journey	safari	journeys	_____	_____
23	simba	lion	simba	lions	_____	_____
24	ɲumba	house	ɲumba	houses	_____	_____
25	ɲuki	bee	ɲuki	bees	_____	_____
26	kikapu	basket	vikapu	baskets	_____	_____
27	kisu	knife	visu	knives	_____	_____
28	kitabu	book	vitabu	books	_____	_____
29	kipini	handle	vipini	handles	_____	_____
30	kiti	stool	viti	stools	_____	_____
31	kitoto	infant	vitoto	infants	_____	_____
32	gari	cart	magari	carts	_____	_____
33	ʃoka	axe	maʃoka	axes	_____	_____
34	kaʃa	cheat	makaʃa	chests	_____	_____
35	d͡ʒembe	hoe	mad͡ʒembe	hoes	_____	_____
36	boga	pumpkin	maboga	pumpkins	_____	_____

Swahili nouns fall into a number of classes, each of which has a characteristic method of forming the singular and the plural. In addition, these noun classes have great significance in the syntax; this will be examined in Problem 4.13 on KiSwahili syntax. Five of the noun classes are illustrated in the data above.

a. Examine the five groupings of nouns. List the prefixes for each word in the spaces provided to the right of the words. For example, for nouns 1–5 list /m- ⌒ wa-/ as the prefixes. If there is no discernible prefix in a group, use a zero {Ø-} prefix. You will probably want to use a zero prefix for the singular items in lines 32–36.

b. List all of the stems in the spaces provided. Is it possible to determine the stem in every case? Why not? What words give you the most trouble? Explain the kind of trouble you encounter in determining stems and prefixes. What other words from the list might help you to determine the correct stems in these cases? Are those words all in the same noun classes? If not, what does this suggest to you about the possible semantics of the different prefixes?

c. Transfer the prefixes from the spaces above to the first five lines of the chart below. Be careful to keep the same order as in the data. For example, list /m-/ and /wa-/ as singular and plural, respectively, for class number 1. The nouns from Exercise 4.11 should be included in the chart as class 6. Use a capital letter {U-} to indicate the two different singular prefixes from that class. Use a capital letter {N-} to indicate all of the different plural prefix allomorphs for that class. {N-} is a convenient way to sum up the kind of homorganic phonetic pattern that you found in that exercise; that is, {N-} means /m-/ in the context Nb, /n-/ in the context Nd, and so on. This abbreviation is convenient because similar morphophonemic variation occurs elsewhere in Swahili. You can also use {N-} to indicate the singular and plural patterns in class 3.

	Singular Prefixes	Plural Prefixes
Class 1	/m-/	/wa-/
Class 2		
Class 3		
Class 4		
Class 5		
Class 6	{U-}	{N-}

4.13   KiSwahili Syntax

The following groups of sentences and phrases are arranged into substitution frames. Each sentence or phrase is numbered to match the numbers of the noun classes in the KiSwahili exercises above. For example, A1 represents noun class number 1, A2 matches noun class number 2, and so on. As you examine each group you will notice that as the nouns change, so do certain other parts of the sentence or phrase. For example, if you compare sentences A1 and A5, you will see that where the "head" noun is *mtu* 'person,' the following word takes the form of *mzuri*, but where the "head" noun is *gari* 'car,' the following word takes the form of *zuri*. This kind of noun-class "agreement" pattern is common in all Bantu languages. It is sometimes called a "concord" system. If you compare all of the sentences in group A with one another, you should be able to identify all of the different words and to sort out how they are changing. Look for more detailed instructions following.

A1	mtu	mzuri	mmod͡ʒa	yule	ameaŋguka	That one good person fell down.
A2	ʃale	mzuri	mmod͡ʒa	ule	umeaŋguka	arrow
A3	ŋgoma	nzuri	mod͡ʒa	ile	imeaŋguka	drum
A4	kikapu	kizuri	kimod͡ʒa	kile	kimeaŋguka	basket
A5	gari	zuri	mod͡ʒa	lile	limeaŋguka	cart
A6	ubao	mzuri	mmod͡ʒa	ule	umeaŋguka	plank

B1	watu	wazuri	wawili	wale	wameaŋguka	Those two good people fell down.
B2	miʃale	mizuri	miwili	ile	imeaŋguka	arrows
B3	ŋgoma	nzuri	mbili	zile	zimeaŋguka	drums
B4	vikapu	vizuri	viwili	vile	vimeaŋguka	baskets
B5	magari	mazuri	mawili	yale	yameaŋguka	carts
B6	mbao	nzuri	mbili	zile	zimeaŋguka	planks

C1	anamtaka	mtoto	mdogo	waŋgu	He wants my little child.
C2	anautaka	mzigo	mdogo	waŋgu	load
C3	anaitaka	ndizi	ndogo	yaŋgu	banana
C4	anakitaka	kisu	kidogo	tʃaŋgu	knife
C5	analitaka	ʃoka	dogo	laŋgu	axe
C6	anautaka	ufuŋguo	mdogo	waŋgu	key
D1	anawataka	watoto	wadogo	waŋgu	He wants my little children.
D2	anaitaka	mizigo	midogo	yaŋgu	loads
D3	anazitaka	ndizi	ndogo	zaŋgu	bananas
D4	anavitaka	visu	vidogo	vyaŋgu	knives
D5	anayataka	maʃoka	madogo	yaŋgu	axes
D6	anazitaka	fuŋguo	ndogo	zaŋgu	keys
E1	unampenda	mpiʃi	mrefu	yupi	Which tall cook do you like?
E2	unaupenda	mti	mrefu	upi	tall tree
E3	unaipenda	pʰembe	ndefu	ipi	long horn
E4	unakipenda	kipini	kirefu	kipi	long handle
E5	unalipenda	dʒembe	refu	lipi	long hoe
E6	unaupenda	uwati	mrefu	upi	long pole
F1	unawapenda	wapiʃi	warefu	wapi	Which tall cooks do you like?
F2	unaipenda	miti	mirefu	ipi	tall trees
F3	unazipenda	pʰembe	ndefu	zipi	long horns
F4	unavipenda	vipini	virefu	vipi	long handles
F5	unayapenda	madʒembe	marefu	yapi	long hoes
F6	unazipenda	mbati	ndefu	zipi	long poles
G1	ninawapata	watoto	wazuri	watatu	wenu	I am getting your three fine children.
G2	ninaipata	mikufu	mizuri	mitatu	yenu	chains
G3	ninazipata	kʰuku	nzuri	tʰatu	zenu	chickens
G4	ninavipata	vitabu	vizuri	vitatu	vyenu	books
G5	ninayapata	makaʃa	mazuri	matatu	yenu	chests
G6	ninazipata	pʰanga	nzuri	tʰatu	zenu	swords
H1	mtoto	mkubwa	wa	mtu mrefu	yule	that tall man's large child
H2	mti	mkubwa	wa	mtu mrefu	yule	tree
H3	ɲumba	kʰubwa	ya	mtu mrefu	yule	house
H4	kisu	kikubwa	tʃa	mtu mrefu	yule	knife
H5	kaʃa	kubwa	la	mtu mrefu	yule	chest
H6	upindi	mkubwa	wa	mtu mrefu	yule	bow

I1	watoto	wadogo	watano	wa	mdʒeni	yupi	Which stranger's five small children?
I2	miʃale	midogo	mitano	ya	mdʒeni	yupi	arrows
I3	kʰamba	ndogo	tʰano	za	mdʒeni	yupi	ropes
I4	vikapu	vidogo	vitano	vya	mdʒeni	yupi	baskets
I5	maʃoka	madogo	matano	ya	mdʒeni	yupi	axes
I6	ɲembe	ndogo	tʰano	za	mdʒeni	yupi	razors

J1	watu	waliwataka	wapagazi	wakubwa	wote	The men wanted all the big porters.
J2	watu	waliitaka	mikufu	mikubwa	yote	chains
J3	watu	walizitaka	ŋgoma	kʰubwa	zote	drums
J4	watu	walivitaka	vitabu	vikubwa	vyote	books
J5	watu	waliyataka	madʒembe	makubwa	yote	hoes
J6	watu	walizitaka	ɲavu	kʰubwa	zote	nets

a. Identify the words in each sentence by comparing whole sentences just as you have been comparing words to identify morphemes. For example, if you compare *mtu mzuri mmoja* 'one good person' of sentence A1 with *watu wazuri waili* 'two good people' of sentence A2, you should be able to determine that *moja* is 'one' and *waili* is 'two' and therefore that *mzuri* must be 'good.' Continue comparing sentences and phrases to identify all of the words. Write the English equivalent for each column of words below that column. For example, under the *mzuri, nzuri, kizuri* (etc.) column, write the English word 'good,' under the *mmoja, moja, kimoja* (etc.) column write the English word 'one,' under the *wawili, miwili, mbili* column in group B write the English word 'two,' and so on for all words in the data.

b. Identify the nouns. Draw a circle around each group of nouns. Notice how each noun is composed of a prefix plus a stem (don't forget about "zero," or silent, prefixes). Write the prefixes for the different noun classes into the chart on the next page. (Do not write the noun stems into the chart.)

c. Identify the verbs. You should be able to recognize them—and their components—by consulting the KiSwahili Verbs exercise. Draw a square around each group of verbs. Recall how the verbs include information about subject, tense, and object, as well as action. The stem identifies the action; the prefixes contain the rest of the information. Now pay attention to how the subject and object prefixes change to "agree" with each different noun class. Identify the subject and object prefixes used with each noun class and write them into the chart on the next page.

d. Think of all of the other words in this exercise—everything that is neither a noun nor a verb—as adjectives. Notice how all of these adjectives fall into three subclasses. Some are adjectives of "quality," others are adjectives of "quantity," and still others are "demonstrative" (or "deictic") adjectives (English words 'this' and 'that') or "possessive" adjectives ('my' and 'your'). As with the nouns, each adjective is constructed from a prefix and a stem. Identify all of the stems and prefixes and list them in the chart on the next page. First list the different prefixes for each subclass of adjectives. Below each group of prefixes list the adjective stems that go with that set of prefixes. Don't be confused by the variation you find in the prefixes; it should be familiar to you from your work with the KiSwahili Nouns and Noun Classes exercises.

THE CONCORD SYSTEM OF SWAHILI

Nouns		Verbs		Adjectives		
		Subject	Object	Subclass 1	Subclass 2	Subclass 3
Singular						
Class 1						
Class 2						
Class 3						
Class 4						
Class 5						
Class 6						
Plural						
Class 1						
Class 2						
Class 3						
Class 4						
Class 5						
Class 6						
Adjective stems						

e. Make a brief statement concerning KiSwahili syntax. What is the order of words in a sentence or phrase? What is the order of Subject, Object, and Verb in a KiSwahili sentence? Which prefixes seem to agree with which nouns? If there are two different nouns in a single sentence, how do you know which prefixes to use with which nouns?

f. Translate the following English sentence into Swahili:

That big child wants those men's three long knives.

4.14 English Newspaper Headlines

Here are some actual sentences from newspaper headlines in the United States. Each is ambiguous because it has more than one possible underlying structure. For each sentence it should be possible to illustrate the underlying structures by drawing syntactic trees or by labeling alternative substitution frames. Your instructor will tell you which sentences you should analyze:

"Include Your Children When Baking Cookies"
"Eye Drops Off Shelf"
"Squad Helps Dog Bite Victim"
"Enraged Cow Injures Farmer With Axe"

4.15 Your Own Language

In the space below, write an ambiguous sentence from each language that you speak. Use the same analytic techniques (syntactic trees, substitution frames) to reveal the underlying structures for each of the sentences that you provide.

◈ WEB EXERCISES

4.1 Go to the companion website for a set of links to additional readings and exercises in morphology and syntax.

4.2   Follow the link on the companion website to the Language Construction Kit. What kinds of grammars are suggested there? How different do they seem from your own grammar?

4.3   Search the InfoTrac database for articles about morphology and syntax.

◈ GUIDED PROJECTS

Language Creating

If your instructor has assigned this project, then this is the time to use your sounds to develop words and sentences. Your instructor will be your guide here, providing details as you need them. As you complete each step in the process, hand in two copies of your group's work. Be sure to include your group's name, as well as the names of all of the individuals present who contributed to the day's work.

Conversation Partnering

If your instructor has assigned this project, you may be asked to compare and analyze similarities and differences in word order and/or sentence structure between your conversation partner's language and your own. Your instructor will provide more details on how to do this.

CHAPTER 5

Language in Action

Note: Your instructor will indicate which readings, exercises, and/or projects you should do.

✳ READING

5.0 "Native American Non-Interference" by Jimm Good Tracks

Jimm Good Tracks's "Native American Non-Interference" is an impassioned plea to social workers to consider adjusting their conversation styles when working with Native Americans. It provides a nice description and contrast of Native American and Anglo-American speaking styles and shows how misunderstandings can result from the mismatch between styles. When he wrote this article Good Tracks, MSW, was a guidance counselor at the Toyei Indian Boarding School in Ganado, Arizona.

> The native American principle of noninterference with others creates
> an obstacle for social workers trying to practice "intervention,"
> but much patience and respect for the principle
> can enable workers to be effective in Indian communities.

The standard techniques and theories of social work that bring positive results with many groups, including lowerclass Anglo-Americans (Anglos), Negroes, and assimilated Mexicans, are not successful when applied to native Americans.[1] In fact, all the methods usually associated with the term "social work intervention" diminish in effectiveness *just to the extent that the subject has retained his native Indian culture*. The reason is that any kind of intervention is contrary to the Indian's strict adherence to the principle of self determination. The less assimilated and acculturated the individual, the more important this principle is to him. Some time ago Wax and Thomas described this principle as noninterference.[2]

Many human relations unavoidably involve some influencing, meddling, and even coercion or force. Indians feel, however, that Anglos carry these elements to an extreme while professing an entirely different set of values. Anglos say they prize freedom, minding one's own business, and the right of each person to decide for himself, yet they also think it right to be their brother's keeper, to give advice and take action to their brother's best interest— as interpreted by the Anglo, in and by the Anglo social context.

In native Indian society, however, no interference or meddling of any kind is allowed or tolerated, even when it is to keep the other person from doing something foolish or dangerous. When an Anglo is moved to be his brother's keeper and that brother is an Indian, therefore, almost everything he says or does seems rude, ill-mannered, or hostile. Perhaps it is the Anglo's arrogant righteousness that prevents him from grasping the nature of his conduct. But if the Indian told the Anglo that he was being intrusive, the Indian would himself be interfering with the Anglo's freedom to act as he sees fit.

Coercion and Suggestion

Coercion appears to be a fundamental element in the peoples of Western Europe and their colonial descendants. All the governments; and institutions of these societies use a variety of coercive methods to insure cooperative action. Traditional Indian societies, on the other hand, were organized on the principle of voluntary cooperation. They refrained from using force to coerce.

In recent times Euro-American societies have tended to rely less heavily on physical violence, but they have only replaced it with verbal forms of coercion and management. Anglo children appear to be taught by their elders, peer groups, and mass media to influence, use, and manipulate others to achieve their personal goals. They begin to try to manipulate others early in life while at play and in their relationships with adults. They continue to improve their manipulative skill throughout their lives as they study psychology and apply it to marriage counseling and psychotherapy. Their newspapers print "Dear Abby" letters from people who want someone else to tell them what to do or how to make others do as they wish. This ability is rightly called a tool essential for living and achieving success in Anglo society. Anglo economic development and exploitation could not otherwise exist. But even when verbal manipulation has superseded physical force, it still remains a form of coercion and constitutes interference. This does not disturb Anglos who feel there is a distinction.

Even a nondirective teacher utilizes some coercion when he wants his pupils to acquire a certain skill, express themselves with certain prepared materials, or participate in a group activity. It appears that the compulsion to interfere is so habitual among Anglos that even when they have no particular business to accomplish in a conversation, they will still tend to be coercive. For instance, one person may remark that he wishes to buy a new car. Someone will immediately tell him where he should buy one and perhaps what kind. In the most friendly manner Anglos are always telling each other and everyone else what they should do, buy, see, sell, read, study, or accomplish—all without any consideration of what the individual may want to do.

But whether it is a subtle suggestion or an outright command, it is considered improper behavior and an interference by Indian people. The Indian child is taught that complete noninterference in interaction with all people is the norm, and that he should react with amazement, irritation, mistrust, and anxiety to even the slightest indication of manipulation or coercion.

Respect and Consideration

The following incident illustrates noninterference in the simplest of matters. I was visiting my cousins when one of them put on his coat and said he was going down town. He had no car, so one could assume he was going to walk. I restated his intention and volunteered to drive him. The cousin showed noninterference with my activities by not asking or even suggesting that I drive him, although that is certainly what he wanted. If he had asked directly and I had not cared to drive him, I would have been put on the spot. I would have been forced to refuse unobligingly or agree unwillingly. But by simply putting on his coat and announcing his intentions, he allowed me to accept or reject his desires without causing bad feelings for anyone. I could volunteer to take him or pay no attention to his actions.

A cross-cultural misunderstanding might occur in the following way. A non-Indian guest at my mother's home, having enjoyed a rice dinner, might pay my mother this compliment: "Your rice was so good! I should be happy to have your recipe, if I may. And do you want some of my rice recipes in exchange?" The offer of recipes might strengthen friendship among Anglos, but to an Indian it cancels the compliment. If my mother had wanted other recipes she would have suggested it to her guest. When the guest makes the offer on her own initiative, it implies she did not really care for my mother's rice and knows a better way to prepare it. If the guest had talked only about various ways of preparing rice, she would have given my mother the opportunity to ask about any that interested her.

An Indian will usually withdraw his attention from a person who interferes. If the ill-mannered person does not take the hint, the Indian will leave. In the event he is unable to leave, he will attempt to fade into the background and become unnoticed. In this way, he will avoid provoking the ill-mannered person to further outbursts and at the same time save the person embarrassment by not witnessing his improper behavior. This reaction also reprimands the one who interferes in a socially sanctioned manner. At such times, an Indian can only wonder at the person and wish he could leave. On occasion, however, when pushed beyond endurance, he may lose his self-control and drive the aggressor away with verbal or physical force.

Much delicacy and sensitivity are required for Indian good manners. If one is planning a gathering, for example, a feast to give a child his Indian name, one does not urge people to come. This would be interfering with their right to free choice. If people wish to come, they will come. Under most ordinary circumstances, an Indian does not even speak to another unless there is some indication that the other desires to turn his attention to him. If one wishes to speak with another, whether it is friend, relative, or spouse, he will place himself in the person's line of vision. If the person's behavior does not indicate an acknowledgment of one's presence, one waits or goes away until later. Should one be talking with a friend and without fore-thought bring up a subject that may be sensitive or distressing to the listener, the latter will look away and pretend not to hear or suddenly change the subject.

The rules of etiquette are generally followed even by many assimilated Indians. They express a deep respect for the interests, responsibilities, and pursuits of other people. The same respect can be seen even in the behavior of young children. They play in the midst of adults who are having a conversation and yet never interrupt. A child may come and lean for a while against his parent or relative, but without a word or act of interference. Only in an emergency does a child try to attract an adult's attention, and then in a way that will not interrupt the adult's activity. A child who gets hurt playing, for example, might come in crying and then go lie down on a bed. The adult hears the crying and decides if he wishes to attend to the child. A bold child who wants something quietly comes up to his parent, stands there a while, and then whispers the request. It seems that even the youngest Indian children do not bother older people when they are preoccupied.

This behavior is taken for granted by Indian people as the proper way to behave. Learning it probably takes place on an unconscious level. Indian infants and those beginning to walk do not make loud attempts to attract their parents' attention as Anglo babies do. This suggests that demanding attention is actually taught the Anglo infant. Indian adults do not respond to interfering demands, so the child does not learn coercive methods of behavior. This does not imply that Indian children are never aggressive, but only that the culture does not reward aggression when it interferes with the activity of others. Indian children are taught to be considerate through the example of their elders, and the adult treats the child with the same respect and consideration that he expects for himself. It is generally against the childrearing practices of Indian people to bother or interrupt their children when they are playing or to make them do something against their will, even when it is in their own best interest. Some Anglo educators show their ignorance of this principle by condemning Indian parents for not forcing their children to attend school.

Implications for Practice

This principle explains much of the general failure of social workers to treat the social and psychological problems of Indian clients. There are other factors, of course, such as the Indian's perception of the worker as an authority figure representing a coercive institution and an alien, dominating, and undesirable culture. The physical appearance of the worker is another factor, and so is his ignorance of the manners of Indian people. The relationships that both client and worker have with the agency make for further complications, but an understanding of the principle of noninterference can still have an important effect on the worker's role. It can teach him what to expect in his social work relationships with Indian clients and thus enable him to be more effective in helping Indian people.

From an Indian client's viewpoint, the worker is expected to perform only the superficial and routine administrative functions of his office. Clients may request him to increase their aid grants, to draw upon some of their own funds from the agency Individual Indian Monies (IIM) accounts, to assist with a government form, or to submit a boarding-school application. These tasks involve no real social involvement, as involvement is understood both by Indians and non-Indians. The Indian client does not allow or desire the worker to have any insight into his inner thoughts. That would not be a proper part of work.

This expectation does not, of course, correspond to the professional social worker's own concept of his function. A worker could become quite frustrated just shuffling papers about and doing little actual social work when there might be plenty of social problems evident among his clientele. Nevertheless, the worker must not intervene unless the people request an intervention, and he is likely to wait a long time for such a request. The credentials of his profession, his position, status, knowledge, skills, achievements, and authority, though respected by the agency, are in most cases completely without merit among the Indians. Such things belong to Anglo culture and are not readily translatable into Indian culture. His standing in the Anglo community does not give him a license to practice intervention among Indian people.

The explanation for the social worker's initial uselessness is easily given. His professional function is generally performed from within the Indian culture, and no foreign interference is desired or contemplated. If a man's problems seem to be a result of his having been witched, for example, he will seek out the properly qualified person to help him alleviate the condition. He will have no need of any outside diagnoses or assistance. Should a personal or family problem be of another nature, it is addressed again to the proper individual, an uncle (mother's brother) or a grandfather—not to a foreigner such as the social worker. In every case, the people utilize the established, functional, culturally acceptable remedy within their own native system.

Worker's Approach

Can a worker ever convey his potential for helpfulness to Indian clients without breaking their norms? How can he do this while they adhere to the principle of noninterference?

Patience is the number-one virtue governing Indian relationships. A worker who has little or no patience should not seek placements in Indian settings. Native temporal concepts are strange to the non-Indian. Some non-Indians even believe these concepts are unstructured and dysfunctional, and perhaps they are—in the Anglo conceptual framework. But the social worker's success may well be linked with his ability to learn "Indian time" and adjust his relationships accordingly.

Native temporal concepts have no relation to the movements of a clock. They deal in terms of natural phenomena—morning, days, nights, months (from the native concept of "moon"), and years (from the native concepts of "seasons" or "winters"). Ignorance of these concepts makes it impossible to understand the long time it takes any alien to become established in the Indian community. For although they are seemingly without interest, perhaps even indifferent to the new worker, the people will at length carefully observe the manner in which he presents and carries himself. It would be well for the worker to know how slow this evaluation process is likely to seem, for he must not become impatient. The evaluation will progress in accordance with native temporal concepts. Perhaps in a year or so a majority of the people will have come to some conclusions about the worker's character. Basic acceptance comes only after there has been enough observation to determine with reasonable assurance that the worker will not inflict injury with his activities.

There is little or nothing the worker may do to expedite the process; to push things along would be interfering with the process and the people. In the meantime, as he performs his superficial functions for the people, he may discreetly interject bits and pieces of his potential for further assistance. But discretion is needed to the utmost in order to avoid the slightest coercive suggestion. If the worker inflicts a coercive tone in conversation and thus thwarts an individual's self-determination, it could be a major setback and perhaps mean complete failure with that individual.

Only time can bring the fruition of the worker's occasional hints. One day a person may decide to test the words of the worker with a real problem. It would not be a preconceived act, discussed before hand in the community, but merely an impulse on the part of one individual to find out the truth of the worker's boasting. Nevertheless, there will be many among the people who are likely to be aware of it.

A great deal may depend upon this trial case, perhaps the entire future relationship between the worker and his clientele. The worker should recognize the importance of this opportunity and be keenly aware of its possible ramifications. A positive solution to the test problem can be the best way to advertise the worker's potential usefulness. A success will travel quickly by word of mouth throughout the close-knit Indian community, and as the good word spreads the worker's worth to the community becomes recognized. Other clients will come forth.

It will never be necessary to perform "social work intervention" and interfere with an individual or the community norms. The people will incorporate the worker into their functional system. He will perform social work in agreement with the native system rather than try to intervene on the basis of a foreign system. Otherwise he would alienate the people.

An alien, it should be noted, is anyone who is not a member of the tribal group. Among Navajos, a Cheyenne would be as alien as an Anglo, though his acceptance may be more readily attainable.

Working within the System

Needless to say, this discussion has excluded numerous complications that are always present in reality, but an effective approach to the noninterference norm is basic to any social work with Indians. If the worker is ever mindful of this norm and how it conditions his role and acceptance, he should be able to deal with the other problems.

A continued adherence to engagement from within the preexisting native framework will assure the confidence and trust of Indian clients. In time they may use the worker to assist with personal problems pertaining to matters outside the native system and even with problems inside the native system that for one reason or another cannot be resolved by the regular native approaches. In the latter case, however, the problem would actually be resolved by a regular approach, inasmuch as the worker would have *become* a native approach by functioning within the native framework.

But even then it should be kept well in mind that the worker is still an alien. The degree of acceptance is based entirely on how well he is able to work within the preexisting native systems and norms. Perfect acceptance comes only with the loss of the worker's alien status, which cannot be achieved except through adoption by Indian people. To become one of the people is, of course, most unlikely, but not impossible.

NOTES

1. The author's experience indicates that the statements made in this article apply to the Navajo and the tribes of the Northern and Southern Plains. Much that is said here might also be true of the Pueblo and other tribes.

2. Wax, Rosalie H., and Robert K. Thomas. "Anglo Intervention vs. Native Noninterference" *Phylon*, 22 (Winter 1961), pp. 53–56.

◈ WRITING/DISCUSSION EXERCISES

5.1 Read Jimm Good Tracks's "Native American Non-Interference." Write a short summary of the article, focusing on how Good Tracks uses the concept of non-interference to describe Native American interactions. Discuss this idea with your classmates. Do you all understand the concept in the same way?

5.2 What does Good Tracks's description of non-interference suggest about possible miscommunication between Native American clients and European American social workers?

5.3   Give an example of a situation in which you have misunderstood a request or an offer because of indirection on either your part or the part of the other person involved. What did you do? What would you do differently now that you understand how indirection works?

5.4   Try your hand at unpacking a Rich Point. Describe the Rich Point in detail, using the S-P-E-A-K-I-N-G rubric. Why was it a Rich Point? What frame-shifting would be necessary for this not to be a Rich Point in the future?

◈ WEB EXERCISES

5.1   Follow the links on the companion website about language in action. Look for sites describing the ethnography of speaking, ethnomethodology, genderlects, and other issues covered in this chapter. Write a short essay summarizing current research in one of these areas.

5.2   Search the InfoTrac database for articles about the ethnography of speaking.

5.3   Search the InfoTrac database for articles about gender, power, and ethnicity in language style.

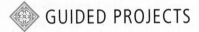 GUIDED PROJECTS

Language Creating

If your instructor has assigned this project, then this is the time to develop a linguistic "style" for your speech community. In addition, you should note or create a social distinction within your group (gender, age, rank, eye color, . . .) and mark it with language (i.e., phonemically or morphologically) or with linguistic style. Your instructor will be your guide here, providing details as you need them. As you complete each step in the process, hand in two copies of your group's work. Be sure to include your group's name, as well as the names of all of the individuals present who contributed to the day's work.

Conversation Partnering

If your instructor has assigned this project, you may be asked to compare and analyze similarities and differences in speaking style between you and your conversation partner. Your instructor will provide more details on how to do this.

CHAPTER 6

Nonverbal Communication

Note: Your instructor will indicate which readings, exercises, and/or projects you should do.

✳ READING

6.0 "Personal Space: The Hidden Element of Cowboy Demeanor" by Joseph V. Hickey and William E. Thompson

Joseph Hickey and William Thompson's "Personal Space: The Hidden Element of Cowboy Demeanor" is a light-hearted yet serious look at proxemics among cowboys in the western Plains region of the United States. Although the authors don't address the question, there is a strong possibility that some of the "demeanor" that Hickey and Thompson describe for cowboys may have been unconsciously borrowed from Plains Indians during the early days of contact between the two groups.

Although cowboy roles have proliferated in the 20th century and today include such specialists as range, feedlot, and rodeo cowboy, all continue to share a common occupation—working with cattle. Cowboys share something else in common that is actually more important to our understandings of the role—it is that cowboys by means of various symbols perform their activities in such a way that all of those with whom they interact recognize them as such. Sociologist Erving Goffman in *Interaction Ritual* defined this as demeanor, "that element of an individual's ceremonial behavior typically conveyed through deportment, dress, and bearing, which serves to express to those in his immediate presence that he is a person of certain desirable or undesirable traits" (1967:77).

Some aspects of cowboy demeanor are today well known. Cowboy dress, for example, has been so popularized by Hollywood and the media, that many elements of cowboy apparel are worn by members of other groups, occupations, and subcultures. Merely wearing the appropriate clothing, however, is not sufficient to make a person a cowboy, for anyone can put on cowboy attire, and "urban cowboys," rural bankers, and others often do. Today, there may, in fact, be more significance in how a cowboy wears his clothing than in what he wears. As Goffman noted in *The Presentation of Self*, "to be a given kind of a person, then, is not merely to possess the required attributes, but also to sustain the standards of conduct and appearance that one's social grouping attaches thereto" (1959:65).

In response to the steady encroachment of mass culture into his symbolic domain, it seems the cowboy has elaborated and embellished a variety of traditional symbols to protect what is his. One of the most effective means he has found in preserving his identity may be his notions of personal space. Borrowed from what appears to be an idealized conception of the old west cowboy as a "rugged individualist," cowboy notions of space have

Source: Joseph V. Hickey and William E. Thompson, "Personal Space: The Hidden Element of Cowboy Demeanor" (1988). Reprinted by permission of the authors.

become so exaggerated and different from those in middle Americans that, at least for now, his social identity seems secure.

Anthropologist Edward Hall distinguished four major distances middle class Americans use in their interactions with others. While each distance is subject to minor adjustments, he noted that the general rules of personal space include: an intimate zone of zero to eighteen inches for loved ones; a personal zone of one and one half to four feet for conversations between people of relatively equal status; a social zone of four to twelve feet for business and social transactions; and a public zone of more than twelve feet that is used by teachers and officials, and in situations where there are considerable status differences among individuals.

While cowboy space, like that of other American subcultures, varies with degree of social relationships, emotion, stress and other factors, the invisible bubble that surrounds the modern cowboy is oversized by typical American standards. The cowboy seems to both literally and figuratively subscribe to the old song verse "Don't Fence Me In." During conversations among cowboys who do not know each other well, the usual speaking distance is between six and eight feet (Hall's social zone). Put another way, the arm's length distance between middle American speakers is stretched by the cowboy to approximately the length of a horse.

Cowboys have found other ways to enlarge their personal territories as well. During our research we found that the cowboy neither stares, nor does he regularly scan the eyes of his partner during conversation. Rather, most of his conversation is spent gazing at his boot tops, at the ground, or towards the open range. The best way to understand proper cowboy eye behavior is to remember the rule that one's gaze must never suggest that one party or another is dominant, or in any way directing a conversation.

Body posture and gestures also serve to enlarge the cowboy's space. The cowboy almost never faces another directly during conversation, and when he does, it can usually be interpreted as a threat. The key to cowboy posture is that it appear as informal and relaxed as possible. Slumped over and casually resting against a fence post or pick-up, the individual attempts to project the ideal image of non-interference.

Cowboys also seem to be particularly adept at using props to enlarge their personal boundaries. Just as women may use purses or the British umbrellas to defend or increase their personal territories, the cowboy employs his own distinctive props. If one observes photos of range cowboys, two of his favorites can sometimes be seen—the campfire and hay bale. Pictures of cowboys around a campfire suggest that they often use campfires to maintain sufficient personal space. Further, it may also allow them to direct their conversations to the fire rather than to each other. It was at a rancher's barbecue that we learned how effective certain props can be. The event was held outdoors near a large central campfire surrounded by hay bale "chairs." Such facilities did not surprise us, but the arrangement of the hay bales did. Rather than positioning them in a neat circle as they might be placed at a girl-scout outing, the rancher had arranged the bales in such a way that not only were they widely spaced, but each was turned slightly away from all others. Unconsciously, the host had placed each hay bale so that none of his guests would have to face another directly.

Other props are also quite effective in boundary maintenance. Cowboys often seem to be busily engaged in a variety of activities even when they are resting or talking to others. They often kick at the ground, pull at the grass, throw small rocks, or pick their teeth with sticks as they talk. All of these activities serve to enhance the cowboy's ideas about personal space and avoidance of eye contact. The pocket knife and chaw of tobacco can serve similar functions. As a cowboy nonchalantly whittles with his knife blade turned outward, chips and shavings tend to fly, making it unwise for another to stand too close. Similarly the chewing of tobacco necessitates a lot of spitting, and whether consciously or unconsciously, this too can be used by the cowboy to enlarge his space.

Possibly the cowboy's favorite prop is his horse. It can be employed in almost every phase of interaction. It is axiomatic that in the Old West, a man and his horse were one, and the same remains somewhat true today. Among range and rodeo cowboys, each individual continues to be measured in part by the quality of his horse and especially how he and his horse function as a team. Ideally, during work, the identities of horse and rider should be indistinguishable. Not surprisingly, this close bond has social correlates. The social distance deemed appropriate for men is equally correct for horses (at least when ridden). When face to face, the acceptable social distance between men on horseback is approximately the length of a horse.

The horse may be such an effective prop because of its versatility. It has behavioral characteristics that can be manipulated by the cowboy to maintain space or to help enter, participate, or even terminate a conversation. On horseback, a cowboy usually shouts to recognize a fellow cowboy while they are widely separated. Each cowboy then slowly ambles over to talk. The horse plays a key role in how the interaction proceeds, for the cowboy often appears to let his horse decide when and where the conversation will take place. Since the horse is both cautious and curious, it moves slowly and carefully forward (just like the cowboy when he enters a conversation), until eventually it settles into a comfortable distance from another's horse. Horse behavior is especially useful in ending a conversation. After standing motionless for awhile, the horse may become restless and move away from the other cowboy's horse. Each cowboy may then allow this distance to grow until it is so large that the cowboys may have to shout their goodbyes.

When not on horseback, cowboy conversation follows other rather special conventions. For the cowboy it seems particularly important that a person appear inconspicuous at the beginning and end of a conversation. Conversations are entered slowly and carefully, and social space is particularly important in projecting the ideal of noninterference. The very beginning of a conversation is usually an abrupt shout from a pick-up window with most relying in kind from a distance of fifty feet or more. During one's approach, it is common for each person to speak in short sentences with considerable pauses allowing the other sufficient time to respond. Longer phrases and the actual purpose of the visit are not broached until each party has settled into a comfortable speaking distance, typically six feet.

Terminating a conversation follows this basic formula in reverse. The most important signal used to end a conversation is the lengthening of space. A student whose father was raised in the Kansas Flint Hills told how it was not uncommon for two cowboys to conclude their conversation from two different locations. For example, two cowboys might carry on a conversation in a man's home. At the conclusion of the visit, the guest begins to move away from his host and towards the front door. The host has two options. He may remain seated while his friend increases the distance between them and eventually exits the house, or he may slowly walk to the screen door and continue the interaction until the visitor enters his pick-up and hits the accelerator. In each case, the participants in the interaction use social distance and even social context (house, truck) to terminate the conversation. The key to a proper performance is that the exit be gradual with each person slowly phasing out the other. First they are dimly seen, then out of sight. Voice level and the substance of conversation are gradually reduced until the conversation has no meaning, or no effect on what another says or thinks. Like the Cheshire cat in Alice in Wonderland's Looking Glass, each cowboy fades away an element at a time.

There appears to be an exception to the exaggerated space that surrounds the cowboy—this is the rule of lateral space. In face-to-face contact, cowboys must maintain a distance of seven feet or more, but side by side this rule does not seem to apply. Laterally, cowboy space is reduced to intimate space (0 to 18″) and they may even touch without violating their rules of social etiquette. It is a common scene at rodeos, or wherever cowboys congregate, to see long rows of cowboys standing or squatting side by side.

Interestingly, in a 1968 cross-national study (Sommer 1968) in which a number of people were asked to rate various seating arrangements, all samples rated side-by-side (or lateral) seating as most intimate. Why this particular space contrasts with cowboys' other ideas of space can only be guessed. One possibility might be that cowboy notions of lateral space are related to jobs they perform. During routine cooperative chores it is common for cowboys to work side by side, periodically bumping and touching. Expansive notions of space here would be so counterproductive that the cowboy could not perform any of his customary chores.

Another possibility may be that cowboy notions of lateral space have been influenced by his favorite companion, the horse. When two cowboys are seated on horses facing each other they would by necessity be approximately a horse length apart. However, side-by-side on horseback, they would be much closer, with perhaps their stirrups even touching. While it would be inexcusable for a cowboy to ride his horse "head on" into another's horse, it is not uncommon at all for their horses to occasionally bump when ridden side-by-side.

It also seems that cowboys place a more exaggerated importance upon backspace than most people. However, practical examples of this social dimension are most difficult to observe. Further, unlike other social distances, the notion of cowboy back space has mythical overtones because the famous Bill Hickok story may make more of this notion of space than actually exists. According to legend, Wild Bill Hickok followed a rule that he never put his back to the door and, of course, the one time that he did not abide by this rule, cost him his life.

What directions cowboy notions of space will take in the future remain uncertain, for the cowboy role, like any social role, is continually being defined and redefined through the process of interaction. Although it is unlikely, cowboy notions of space, like cowboy dress, may one day be coopted by other American groups or occupations, thus forcing the cowboy to make further modifications of this element of his symbolic behavior. At present, cowboys employ notions of space from the cowboy past, but there is no reason this too cannot change. Notions of space may soon be modified by "computer cowboys" who add elements that are more practical in the office or board room than out on the prairie. Of course, it is equally plausible that the opposite may occur. As cowboy specialists become more detached from the range cattle phase of the operation, their notions of space may become even more like that of folk notions of the old west cowboy to compensate for their loss of occupational and cultural ties to the past.

BIBLIOGRAPHY

Blumer, Herbert. *Symbolic Interactionism*. New Jersey, 1969.

Goffman, Erving. *Interaction Ritual*. New York, 1967.

———. *The Presentation of Self in Everyday Life*. New York, 1959.

Hall, Edward. *The Hidden Dimension*. New York, 1966.

———. *The Silent Language*. New York, 1959.

Sommer, R. "Intimacy Ratings in Five Countries." *International Journal of Psychology* 3 (1968), 109–14.

◈ WRITING/DISCUSSION EXERCISES

6.1   Read Hickey and Thompson's "Personal Space: The Hidden Element of Cowboy Demeanor." Write a short summary of the article, focusing on how cowboy proxemics are different from "standard" American proxemics. Discuss these differences with your classmates. Did you all identify the same kinds of differences? What might explain your differences of opinion?

6.2   Give an example of a situation in which you have misunderstood someone else's proxemic system. What did you do? What would you do differently now that you understand how proxemic systems work? Compare your experience with those of other classmates. What perspectives can they add to your analysis? What perspectives can you add to their analyses?

6.3   Give an example of a situation in which you have misunderstood someone else's kinesic system. What did you do? What would you do differently now that you understand how kinesic systems work? Compare your experience with those of other classmates. What perspectives can they add to your analysis? What perspectives can you add to their analyses?

 WEB EXERCISES

6.1   Follow the links on the companion website about kinesics. Write a short essay summing up and evaluating the kinds of information that you find.

6.2 Follow the links on the companion website about proxemics. Write a short essay summing up and evaluating the kinds of information that you find.

6.3 Follow the links on the companion website about sign language. Write a short essay summing up and evaluating the kinds of information that you find.

6.4   Search the InfoTrac database for articles about kinesics and proxemics.

6.5   Search the InfoTrac database for articles about sign language.

◈ GUIDED PROJECTS

Language Creating

If your instructor has assigned this project, then this is the time to develop proxemic and kinesic systems for your speech community. Your instructor will be your guide here, providing details as you need them. As you complete each step in the process, hand in two copies of your group's work. Be sure to include your group's name, as well as the names of all of the individuals present who contributed to the day's work.

Conversation Partnering

If your instructor has assigned this project, you may be asked to compare and analyze similarities and differences in proxemic and kinesic systems between you and your conversation partner. Your instructor will provide more details on how to do this.

CHAPTER 7

Writing and Literacy

Note: Your instructor will indicate which readings, exercises, and/or projects you should do.

✳ READING

7.0 "Spelling Shinzwani: Dictionary Construction and Orthographic Choice in the Comoro Islands" by Harriet Joseph Ottenheimer

Harriet Ottenheimer's "Spelling Shinzwani: Dictionary Construction and Orthographic Choice in the Comoro Islands" focuses a sharp lens on one particular dilemma regarding spelling and unearths a broad range of political and cultural issues. How people spell their language communicates a lot about how they feel about, and choose to signal, their identity with regard to their former colonial rulers and their current independent status. It is important for linguistic anthropologists to be sensitive to these issues. Note that this particular article uses a combination of American (Pike) and IPA phonetic symbols.

1. Introduction

The Comoro Islands are located in the western Indian Ocean, at the northern end of the Mozambique Channel, midway between Mozambique and the Malagasy Republic. The archipelago is comprised of four islands: Ngazidja (or Grande Comore), Nzwani (or Anjouan), Mwali (or Mohéli), and Mayotte (or Maore). A referendum held in the Comoros in December 1974 led to the independence of three of the islands—Ngazidja, Nzwani, and Mwali—from nearly a century of French colonial rule in July 1975, while Mayotte remained connected to France. Today, Ngazidja, Nzwani, and Mwali form the Federal Islamic Republic of the Comoro Islands. The Republic's continuing claim of sovereignty over Mayotte, and the recent attempted secession of Nzwani from the Republic, complicate the political picture.

Located along Indian Ocean maritime trading routes, the Comoros have absorbed a wide variety of linguistic and cultural influences, most notably from Swahili, Arabic, Hindi, Malagasy, Portuguese, English, and French. This influence has not been distributed equally among the islands, however, with the result that there are four different language varieties in the archipelago (see Ottenheimer and Ottenheimer 1976, Nurse 1989, Nurse and Hinnebusch 1993). Each island exhibits a unique blend of lexical and grammatical materials so that mutual intelligibility among the four islands cannot be taken for granted. As Comorian linguist Mohamed Ahmed-Chamanga points out, "the different [language] varieties . . . are divided into two groups: shingazidja-shimwali /shinzwani-shimaore. Within each group mutual intelligibility is quasi-immediate. In contrast, a period of adjustment of some length is necessary between speakers of the different groups." (Ahmed-Chamanga,

Source: "Spelling Shinzwani: Dictionary Construction and Orthographic Choice in the Comoro Islands," by Harriet Joseph Ottenheimer, *Written Language and Literacy* 4, no. 1 (2001), pp. 15–29. With kind permission by John Benjamins Publishing Company, Amsterdam/Philadelphia, www.benjamins.com.

Lafon, & Sibertin-Blanc 1986; translation mine). Nonetheless, today it has become politically convenient to consider all four varieties, somewhat optimistically, as "Comorian."

This paper surveys the history of dictionary construction and orthographic choice in the Comoros with particular reference to the development of the first bilingual, bidirectional Shinzwani-English dictionary. I begin with a brief survey of outsiders' attempts to collect word lists and compile dictionaries of Comorian in general and Shinzwani in particular. After introducing the place of my own linguistic work in the Comoros, which began the 1960s, I then present a history of the various orthographic systems used and/or proposed by Comorians including Arabic, French, English, and phonemic. I conclude with a discussion of the role of the linguistic anthropologist and the importance of sensitivity to context and politics in questions of orthographic choice.

2. European Spellings

The earliest collections of Comorian words come to us from British explorers. In the early 1600s Payton (1613), Roe (1615), and Herbert (1626) wrote down a few words of Shimwali [but note that Herbert's list was the same as Payton's and may have been copied from him, rather than collected in the Comoros]. As might be expected, their transcriptions were improvised on an English orthographic base. Roe, for example, wrote *moschees* for /mše/ 'female' (and gave a gloss of 'women').

Nearly two centuries later, in 1821–22, the Rev. William Elliot took up a two-year residence as a missionary in Mutsamudu, on the island of Nzwani. Elliot collected some 900 words of Shinzwani along with some sample sentences, and struggled with the Bantu grammar. He, too, used an improvised transcription system—which, no doubt, was based on his own English orthographic practices. He wrote *moo-sha* for /mše/ 'female,' for example. Elliot's manuscript was stored away in the Grey Library at Capetown, South Africa, and did not attract attention again until Heepe, a German linguist, rediscovered it and published it with commentary in 1926.

The mid 1800s brought more European word-list collecting in the Comoros. Shinzwani word lists were collected by Peters (some time during 1842–48 and published by Bleek 1856), by Hildebrandt 1875, by Last 1885, and by an unknown Frenchman whose 1856 collection was published by Struck 1909. [In addition, a Shingazidja word list was published by Steere in 1869.]

In 1893, Ormières, a linguistically-inclined colonial administrator in Nzwani, collected and published a list of some 3,000 lexical items in Shinzwani. An early IPA system of transcription might have been available to him, but there is no indication that he used it. Relying on his own French-based orthography he transcribed words like /mše/ 'female' as *mouche*. Ormières' word list was published in 1893 in France, and went out of print soon after.

The next Comorian collection of any size was made either between 1910 and 1914 or during the 1930s—there are conflicting accounts of the timing but the latter date is more likely—by Fr. Sacleux, a French missionary residing in Zanzibar. Relying on his porter, who was from Ngazidja, Sacleux compiled a list of Shingazidja equivalents for French words. He also included some Shinzwani in this collection, having obtained samples through correspondence with M. A. M. Angot, a French planter and amateur linguist residing in Nzwani. Although Sacleux published two Swahili dictionaries (1939–41, 1949), his Shingazidja dictionary was only published posthumously (Ahmed-Chamanga and Gueunier 1979), and it went out of print almost immediately afterward.

In 1939 M. Gex, the Superior Administrator of the Comoros, asked Angot and Fr. Fischer, a French missionary in Ngazidja, to develop a combined dictionary/grammar including all of the principal dialects of the Comoros. As Angot put it, "too great differences in the pronunciation, syntax, and conjugations forced us to renounce the uniting of Grande Comorian and Anjouanese in a single work" (Angot 1948:1; translation mine). Instead Angot published a Shinzwani grammar (1946, 1948), and Fr. Fischer published a French-Shingazidja dictionary/grammar (1949). Interestingly, Angot's orthography departed from earlier French-based spellings with regard to the vowels. The phonological unit /wa/ was now written <wa> rather than <oi> while the vowel /u/ was written <u> rather than <ou>. The voiceless fricative phoneme /š/, however, continued to be written in the French way, as <ch>, while the voiced affricate /ǰ/ was written either as <dj> or <g>. Thus /mše/ 'female' was written *mche* and /njema/ 'good' was written *ngema*. The various spellings of /mše/ 'female' can be seen here:

(1)   Roe (1615)   *moschees* ('women')
      Elliot (1821–22)   *moo-sha*
      Ormières (1893)   *mouche*
      Angot (1949)   *mche*

3. Linguistic Research in the 1960s

In the 1960s, as anthropologist Martin Ottenheimer and I began preparing for anthropological field work in the Comoro Islands, we found that most of these early works on Comorian were difficult to obtain, and in most cases impossible. We were able to obtain some materials through used-and-rare book dealers and we were able to read (and hand-copy) some others in libraries and archives, but most of the materials on language were almost impossible to locate. We did not obtain a copy of Angot's Shinzwani grammar, for example, until several months after we had reached Nzwani. We were therefore unable to learn any Comorian prior to our arrival in the Comoros in the early fall of 1967. To learn as much as we could, we spent several months in Moroni and Itsandra, on the island of Ngazidja, learning Shingazidja; then we settled in Domoni, on the island of Nzwani, to learn Shinzwani and to conduct a longer period of field research. On both islands we conducted our research in predominantly monolingual settings.

As there was no published dictionary of Shinzwani we began compiling materials for one. We worked out the phonological system, established a consistent orthography, and began using it in our field notes as well as for transcriptions of tape-recorded narratives and interviews. We used the American phonetic symbols developed by Kenneth Pike 1947 for most sounds, and symbols from the International Phonetic Alphabet for others (most notably implosive and retroflex stops, and interdental and velar fricatives). We used our field notes and transcriptions to augment the rapidly growing dictionary corpus.

Transcribing by hand posed no problems. However, when we began using a small portable typewriter for the transcriptions we had to make some modifications to our symbol set. Although it was a French typewriter with a few dead key accents (acute, grave, circumflex . . .) it did not have some others such as the háček [ˇ]; nor did it have any IPA symbols. Following English and Swahili models, we began using <sh> for /š/, <ch> for /č/, and <j> for /ǰ/. We chose <zh> for /ž/ based on the fact that it is the voiced equivalent of /š/ and <z> is the voiced equivalent of <s>. We followed French practice in choosing <tr> and <dr> for retroflex /ţ/ and /ḑ/, Swahili practice in choosing <th> and <dh> for /θ/, and /ð/, as well as <gh>, for /ɣ/, and we decided that the allophonic variation between [v] and [β] justified using <v> for both.

When several young Comorians volunteered to help with the transcription of the tape recordings, we instructed them in the use of our modified phonemic orthography. Of all the symbols we chose, the English and Swahili-based <sh ch zh j> (which are the focus of this paper) appeared to cause the most difficulty for our young assistants. Those who had been through the French-based public school system were used to using <ch> for the /š/ sound, not <sh>. Additionally, the French spelling for /č/ was either <tsh> or <tsch> but not <ch>. Finally, in the French system the letter <j> represented the sound /ž/, which was common to both Shinzwani and to French. This meant that /ǰ/ was written as <dj> by the French and not as <j>. The possibilities for confusion were high. Nonetheless, our young assistants found they were able to switch back and forth between their French-influenced sense of orthography and our Swahili- and English-based modified phonemic orthography. The differences are shown in Table 1.

TABLE 1

	/š/	/č/	/ž/	/ǰ/
French	ch	t(s)ch	j	dj
Swahili	sh	ch	Ø	j
Ottenheimer 1966	sh	ch	zh	j

4. Dictionaries and Orthographic Choice

After we returned to the United States I continued to maintain the dictionary as a language-retention device, as well as for analytic purposes. I transformed my paper slip file of 1,000 entries to a looseleaf notebook format; and as I continued translating field notes and narratives I added more words to the notebook, inserting and recopying pages as necessary. By the early 1980s the notebook contained nearly 6,000 entries. I also had developed an English-Shinzwani index. In 1982 I brought a photocopy of the notebook to the Comoros along with a chart of noun classes and concords that I had developed. I was stunned by the reaction. The most common comment I heard was something like, "We really *do* have a language (or: a grammar)! The French told us we just spoke gibberish" (or: ". . . we had no grammar"; or: ". . . we didn't have a real language"). Many individuals (including some Comorian government officials) urged me to consider publishing the dictionary.

This idea raised important questions regarding orthography. Up until this point, the Shinzwani dictionary had been an "internal document," intended primarily for my own analytic purposes. The modified phonemic orthography I had developed in the 1960s was well-suited to my rather specific needs. Whether it would work as well for a general Comorian audience was unknown. I knew it had worked for my young transcribers, but I also knew that those who had been to French-based schools had encountered some initial difficulty.

There is a complex interrelationship between publication of language materials and the development of national orthographies (see Tabouret-Keller et al. 1997). In choosing an orthography for a published Shinzwani Dictionary I wanted to be sensitive to these wider linguistic, cultural, and political issues. I wanted to balance my academic concern for linguistic correctness with a practical concern for readability. I wanted to balance the political implications of developing a dictionary and orthography for just one of the linguistic varieties in the Comoros, on the one hand, with an oft-stated Comorian concern for national unification, on the other hand.

With these thoughts in mind, I returned to Kansas, secured NEH funding for the project, and acquired LEXWARE, a flexible linguistic database program which would allow me to prepare a bilingual, bidirectional dictionary for publication—and, up until the last stages of preparing camera-ready copy, would allow me to experiment with a range of orthographic possibilities. This flexibility, as it turns out, has been essential.

5. Choosing Scripts, Choosing Spellings

Shinzwani has been written locally for hundreds of years using Arabic script. Because every child attends Koranic school, literacy in Shinzwani among Shinzwani speakers can be documented to be above 90% (Ahmed-Chamanga and Geunier 1977a:46), and Arabic script is often used for personal letter-writing among speakers of Shinzwani. Recognizing this widespread level of literacy, the French National Assembly passed a resolution in October of 1974 requiring that the bill to organize a referendum for independence in the Comoros should be published not only in French but also in "the most commonly employed local language" (Ahmed-Chamanga and Gueunier 1977b; translation mine). As the population of Ngazidja was larger than that of any of the other islands in the archipelago,

Shingazidja was chosen as "the most commonly employed local language." In addition, Arabic script was to be used for the publication of the referendum in Shingazidja. The documents were translated into Shingazidja (and prepared in Arabic script) by three individuals—a journalist, a member of the Comorian delegation to Paris, and a teacher at the Paris-based National Institute of Oriental Languages and Civilizations (INALCO)—in time for the December 22, 1974 referendum (Ahmed-Chamanga & Gueunier 1977b:217). This experience encouraged the beginnings of local attempts to standardize Arabic script for Comorian. One such project (that of Kamar-Eddine) was to have been documented in an article written by Michel Lafon which was to have been published in the 1980s, but to date the article has not appeared.

Shinzwani has more phonemes than Arabic and certain adjustments are generally made by Comorians as they apply Arabic script to writing their language(s). For example, just two Arabic graphemes are used for the four sounds under discussion in this paper. The Arabic letter *shiin* (ش) is used for both /š/ and /č/; and the Arabic letter *jiim* (ج) is used for both /ž/ and /ǰ/.

Today there are still no fixed conventions for using Arabic script for Comorian. Individual writers must decide on their own which characters to use for which sounds. The following example, in a tape-recorded folktale transcribed by a Shinzwani speaker, shows *jiim* used for both /ž/ and /ǰ/:

(2)   Arabic script: مح امجب اب قجو

       Phonemic transcription: /mahe amǰibu amba kažua/

       English translation: 'His mother answered him that she didn't know.'

Some French colonial planters and government officials had used French to write personal and place names; their influence can be seen, for example, in the spelling of place names on maps of the Comoros. For the most part, however, French spelling was not widely used by Wanzwani. French does not fit Shinzwani much better than Arabic, although it does have separate letter combinations for /š č ž ǰ/.

The Comoros declared their independence from France in July of 1974, under the leadership of Ahmed Abdallah. Within a month the newly independent state was overthown in a coup led by Ali Soilihi. Soon after this, a few young Comorian intellectuals suggested that the Comoros needed a new Latin-based orthography—one that would be more like Swahili than like French (Abdushakur Aboud p.c., Ahmed-Chamanga 1976, Lafon and Sibertin-Blanc 1976). Such a move would symbolize liberation from French colonial influence. French spelling might be appropriate for French, they argued, but the Comoros should have their own orthography, and it should resemble that used in other independent African nations. As Ahmed-Chamanga said, "Being a matter of a practical proposal, and not a theoretical study, we will begin with standard Swahili, a language very close to the different Comorian language varieties, and with which they have direct relationships. We will also adopt new conventions for phonemes not represented . . . in Swahili" (Ahmed-Chamanga 1976; translation mine).

Two different orthographies were proposed: one by Ali Soilihi and one by Ahmed-Chamanga. Both looked a bit like what I had taught the Wanzwani students to use in the 1960s. In both, /š/ was to be spelled with <sh> as in Swahili, rather than with <ch> as in French. In Ali Soilihi's system, however, /ǰ/ would be spelled with <j> (as in Swahili); but /č/ would be spelled with <c>, rather than with the Swahili <ch>. In Ahmed-Chamanga's system, by contrast, /č/ would be written <ch> as in Swahili; but the voiced variants would follow French orthographic practice, so that /ž/ would continue to be spelled with <j>, and /ǰ/ would be spelled with the French combination <dj>; see Table 2.

The two orthographies are an interesting mix of Swahili and French orthographic influences. It is not clear why Ali Soilihi adopted Swahili <sh> and <j> but rejected Swahili <ch> and introduced <c> instead. Nor is it clear why Ahmed-Chamanga adopted Swahili <sh> and <ch> but rejected Swahili <j> in favor of French <dj>. In any case, both or-

TABLE 2

	/š/	/č/	/ž/	/ǰ/
French	ch	t(s)ch	j	dj
Swahili	sh	ch	—[a]	j
Ottenheimer 1966	sh	ch	zh	j
Ali Soilihi 1976	sh	c	—[b]	j
Ahmed-Chamanga 1976	sh	ch	j	dj

[a]Sound not existent in Swahili
[b]Symbol unknown

thographies appear to have fallen into disuse after Ali Soilihi was deposed (by Ahmed Abdallah) in 1978. Perhaps they were too new—or too different. Arabic script continued to be widely used by Comorians for writing Comorian, and those individuals who had been educated in French-style schools reverted to French-based orthographic choices whenever it was necessary to use Latin characters for Comorian. Today some individuals recall using <c> for /č/, but no one seems to recall whether there was a symbol for /ž/ in Ali Soilihi's system.

6. Negotiating Standards

Soon after my 1982 visit to the Comoros, the Comorian government commissioned a linguistic study designed to develop an official Latin-based orthography for Comorian and to "increase literacy" in the Comoros. The resulting orthography, published in 1986 by Moinaecha Cheikh 1986a, b, maintained the English-Swahili style <sh> for /š/, which had been proposed in the 1976 orthographies; however it reverted to the more French-based <tsh> for /č/. The voiced phonemes /ž/ and /ǰ/ also continued to use French spellings (as in Ahmed-Chamanga 1976). Although Moinaecha Cheikh's goal had been to emphasize the underlying unity between the different language varieties in the Comoros, in fact her orthography reflected Shingazidja better than Shinzwani. She proposed using the letter <j> for /ž/—a sound which is present in Shinzwani, but not functional in Shingazidja. However, the rest of the characters and symbols she suggested reflected an emphasis on the sounds and patterns of Shingazidja such as <pv> for both /β/ and [v]. (The orthographically simpler <v> would have been sufficient for Shinzwani.)

It is therefore probably no surprise that her orthography was widely adopted for Shingazidja but not for Shinzwani. It was used in the French-Shingazidja dictionary of Lafon 1991a, b, which was published a few years later; and it is used today in the Comorian-language version (largely Shingazidja) of Al Watwan, the nation's major newspaper, published in Moroni.

The rejection of Moinaecha Cheikh's orthography by Wanzwani may also reflect the deeper ethnic, historical, and political divide that continues to exist between Shinzwani and Shingazidja speakers. Although it may not have been his intent, Ahmed-Chamanga unwittingly seems to have contributed to widening this underlying rift when he introduced, also in 1986, a proposal of his own which argued for a multi-layered approach to orthographic choice in the Comoros (Ahmed-Chamanga, Lafon, & Sibertin-Blanc 1986). One could, he reasoned develop a common set of characters for those sounds which were the same in the two language groups, and different sets of unique but non-overlapping characters for sounds which were unique to each different language variety. Thus /č/ could be written <ch> in Shinzwani, and <tsh> in Shingazidja, with no resulting confusion; see Table 3. Likewise one could write <pv> for /β/ in Shingazidja, but in Shinzwani, where the

TABLE 3

	/š/	/č/	/ž/	/ǰ/
Ahmed-Chamanga 1976	sh	ch	j	dj
Cheikh 1986	sh	tsh	j	dj
Ahmed-Chamanga 1986	sh	ch/tsh	j	dj

equivalent sound was sometimes [v] and sometimes [β], and the difference was not phonemic, <v> would suffice and be less confusing.

From a linguistic standpoint, this made sense, and this is what many Wanzwani have adopted when they write Shinzwani using Latin characters. Nonetheless, in 1992 Ahmed-Chamanga published a Shinzwani-French Dictionary in which he used <tsh> rather than <ch> for /č/. Perhaps the increasing fragility of the Comorian ideal of unity, linguistically as well as politically, contributed to this decision. (However, he did not adopt the Shingazidja <pv>.) Various spellings of /š č ž ǰ/ through time are shown in Table 4.

In 1995, with the situation still in flux, I brought a bound, computer-printed, copy of the Shinzwani-English dictionary to the Comoros for a field test. I was particularly concerned to know how Wanzwani were now reading and writing /š č ž ǰ/. By now nearly all Wanzwani in their 20s have completed at least eight years in local French-style schools, many have completed lycée, and some have studied (or are currently studying) abroad. Working with a range of individuals from young schoolchildren to forty- and fifty-year-old adults, and from housewives to fishermen to schoolteachers, I reviewed the four sounds in terms of their phonetic and graphic interrelationships. I drew phonetic charts, explained the voiced/voiceless and fricative/affricate distinctions, and compared the phonetic, French, and English symbols for the sounds. The discussions were interesting. Most people responded by saying that it really didn't matter, since they were used to reading so many different languages and spellings. If I would just indicate somewhere what symbols were to stand for what sounds, they would adjust as necessary. Pushed to think about what they would really want to see and use, and how they would really want to have the language look on the printed page, most individuals decided that although they liked the English/Swahili <sh> for /š/ and <ch> for /č/, they also preferred the French <j> for /ž/ and <dj> for /ǰ/. This

TABLE 4

	/š/	/č/	/ž/	/ǰ/
Arabic	ش	ش	ج	ج
French	ch	t(s)ch	j	dj
Swahili	sh	ch	Ø	j
Ottenheimer 1966	sh	ch	zh	j
Ali Soilihi 1976	sh	c	?	j
Ahmed-Chamanga 1976	sh	ch	j	dj
Cheikh 1986	sh	tsh	j	dj
Ahmed-Chamanga 1986	sh	ch/tsh	j	dj
Ahmed-Chamanga 1992	sh	tsh	j	dj
Peace Corps 1994	sh	ch	j	dj

is an interesting mix, as it resembles Ahmed-Chamanga's earlier orthography (1986) more than his later one (1992).

I decided to ask some English speakers for reactions as well, so I polled a few of the Peace Corps volunteers in the Comoros, and—later on—some American students in Kansas. As might be expected, the discussions were a bit different. By 1994 one of the Peace Corps workers had developed a small Shingazidja-English dictionary; he was using the English/Swahili <sh> and <ch> for the voiceless pair of sounds, and the French <j> and <dj> for the voiced pair. (It is interesting that <j> was specified at all, since the sound [ž] is used in Shinzwani but not in Shingazidja, which was the target language of the Peace Corps Dictionary.) In spite of this the Peace Corps workers, as well as the American students in Kansas, preferred using the letter <j> for /ǰ/; they felt that using <dj> for the sound was unnecessarily cluttered. However, the combination <zh> for /ž/ was unfamiliar and confusing to them. As a result, they, like the Wanzwani, ended up settling on Chamanga's 1986 orthography as providing the clearest set of choices. For some of them, knowledge that the Comoros had been a French colony affected their choice. "If you know you are dealing with a French-influenced country, you kind of expect to see some French spelling," said one student. Finally, I put out a query to any and all Comorians and former Peace Corps volunteers who were subscribed to an English-speaking Comorian listserve, recently established by Comorians in the United States. With the exception of one individual who recalled having learned Ali Soilihi's 1976 Swahili-based orthography, and who still preferred using <j> for /ǰ/, everyone who responded to me endorsed the use of English/Swahili <sh> and <ch> for /š č /, and French <j> and <dj> for /ž ǰ/.

7. *Wider Implications*

In the summer of 1997 the island of Nzwani seceded from the Federal Islamic Republic of the Comoro Islands. As of this writing a peaceful resolution to this highly charged political situation has not been found. Clearly with the current political situation in the Comoros, much more is at stake than a simple spelling choice. In this case, as perhaps in many more cases around the world than we are aware, the choice of orthography for a dictionary—and the publication of that dictionary—have political implications that go beyond straightforward linguistic choice. If, for example, I follow contemporary Nzwani preference (and Ahmed-Chamanga 1986), then the Shinzwani-English dictionary will help to emphasize the underlying differences between Shinzwani and Shingazidja. If, on the other hand, I follow Ahmed-Chamanga 1992 (and ignore contemporary practice), then the dictionary could help to emphasize the underlying similarities between the language varieties known as Comorian.

Working with Wanzwani speakers on the Shinzwani-English Dictionary provides important insights into orthography and the politics of representation. The complex interplay of orthography, identity, and choice in this small African nation are instructive. An understanding of the dynamics involved can provide us with a model for understanding similar choices on a broader scale; and it can also help us to design and to predict the success of culturally and politically sensitive literacy programs.

8. *Conclusion*

Responsible linguists and linguistic anthropologists must fully understand these variables and their potential role in the process. Linguistic data will always need to be transcribed with as much accuracy as the ear permits and good phonetic data will always be essential to good phonemic analysis. Getting from phonemic to graphemic representation, however, is not as straightforward as it might seem. Orthographic representation must go beyond linguistic analysis to take a much wider set of concerns into account—including history, cultural concerns, and the politics of national and ethnic identity. As Bill Powers has written (1990:497), "any attempt to [impose linguistic rigor on native languages] should be seen as another form of patronization as well as linguistic hegemony. . . . The politics of orthography is not a theoretical idea, it is a reality, one which must be understood and assessed by all those involved with native languages." The decisions we make, as linguists and linguistic anthropologists, in representing individuals and their languages, have far-reaching implications. Understanding these implications is essential.

REFERENCES

Ahmed-Chamanga, Mohamed. 1976. Proposition pour une écriture standard du Comorien. *Asie du Sud-Est et Monde Insulindien* 7(2–3): 73–80.

———. 1992. *Lexique Comorien (Shindzuani)-Français*. Paris: L'Harmattan.

Ahmed-Chamanga, Mohamed, and Noël Jacques Gueunier. 1977a. Récherches sur l'instrumentalisation du Comorien: Les problèmes de graphie d'après la version Comorienne de la loi du 23 Novembere 1974. *Asie du Sud-Est et Monde Insulindien* 8(3–4): 45–77.

———. 1977b. Récherches sur l'instrumentalisation du Comorien: Problèmes d'adaptation lexicale (d'après la version comorienne de la loi du 23 novembre 1974). *Cahiers d'Études Africaines* 17(66–67): 213–239.

———. 1979. *Le dictionnaire Comorien-Français et Français-Comorien du R. P. Sacleux*. Langues et Civilisations de L'Asie du Sud-Est et du Monde Insulindien: Langues, Cultures et Sociétés de l'Ocean Indien. No. 9. Paris: SELAF (Société d'Études Linguistiques et Anthropologiques de France).

Ahmed-Chamanga, Mohamed, Michel Lafon, and Jean-Luc Sibertin-Blanc. 1986. Projet d'orthographe pratique du Comorien. *Études Océan Indien* 9:7–33.

Angot, M. A. M. 1946. Grammaire anjouanaise. *Bulletin de l'Académie Malgache*. Nouvelle Série. 27:89–123.

———. 1948. *Grammaire anjouanaise*. Tananarive: Imprimerie Moderne de l'Émyrne, Pitot de la Beaujardière & Cie.

Cheikh, Moinaecha. 1986a. Essai d'orthographe du comorien. Mimeographed paper, Linguistic Department, *Centre National de Documentation et de Récherche Scientifique (CNDRS)*, Moroni: Comoro Islands (21 pp.).

———. 1986b. Exposés presenté par Mme CHEIKH Moinaecha sur l'initiation à la transcription de la langue comorienne, suivis des synthèses des travaux de groups. Pp. 45–84 of mimeographed study conducted at CNDRS (Centre National de Documentation et de Récherche Scientifique), Moroni: Comoro Islands.

Elliot, W. [1821–22] 1926. A grammar and vocabulary of the Hinzuan language. In M. Heepe, Darstellung einer Bantusprache aus den Jahren 1821–22. *Mitteilungen des Seminars für Orientalische Sprachen an der Friedrich-Wilhelms Universität zu Berlin* 29(3): 199–232.

Fischer, P. François. 1949. *Grammaire-dictionnaire comorien*. Strasbourg: Société d'Editions de la Basse-Alsace.

Heepe, M. 1920. Die Komorendialekte Ngadidja, Nzwani, und Mwali. *Abhanlungen des Hamburgischen Kolonialinstituts* 23:1–166.

———. 1926. Darstellung einer Bantusprache aus den Jahren 1821–22. *Mitteilungen des Seminars für Orientalische Sprachen an der Friedrich-Wilhelms Universität zu Berlin* 29(3): 191–232.

Herbert, Thomas. [1626, 1634, 1677] 1906–1920. Some years travels into divers parts of Africa and Asia the great. In A. Grandidier, G. Grandidier, and H. Froidevaux, *Collection des Ouvrages Anciens Concernant Madagascar*. Paris: Comité de Madagascar, pp. 397–398.

Hildebrandt, J. M. 1875. Material zum wortschatz der johanna-sprache. *Zeitschrift für Ethnologie* 8:89–96.

Lafon, Michel. 1991a. Lexique français-shingazidja. *Travaux et documents du Centre d'Études et de Recherche sur l'Océan Indien*

(CEROI) 14. Paris: Institut National des Langues et Civilizations Orientales (INALCO).

———. 1991b. *Lexique Français-Comorien (Shingazidja)*. Paris: L'Harmattan.

Lafon, Michel, and Jean-Luc Sibertin-Blanc. 1976. Propositions pour une graphie du comorien. Mimeograph. Moroni, Comoro Islands.

Last, J. [1885] 1920. *Polyglotta Africana Orientalis*. London. In M. Heepe, Die Komorendialekte Ngadidja, Nzwani, und Mwali. *Abhanlungen des Hamburgischen Kolonialinstituts* 23:1–166.

Nurse, Derek. 1989. Is Comorian Swahili? Being an examination of the diachronic relationship between Comorian and coastal Swahili. In M-F. Rombi (ed.), *Le Swahili et ses limites. Ambiguité des notions reçues*. Table ronde internationale du CNRS (Sèvres, 20–22 avril 1983). Paris: Editions Récherche sur les Civilisations, pp. 83–105.

Nurse, Derek, and Thomas J. Hinnebusch. 1993. *Swahili and Sabaki: A linguistic history* (Linguistics, vol. 121). Berkeley and London: University of California Press.

Ormières, R. 1893. *Lexique français-anjouanais*. Paris: Imprimerie Polyglotte Hugonis.

Ottenheimer, Harriet Joseph. 1986. *Shinzwani-English dictionary with English-Shinzwani finderlist*. Manhattan, KS: SASW/Comorian Studies, on diskette, 596,000 bytes; 6,000 entries.

———. 1998. *Shinzwani-English dictionary with English-Shinzwani finderlist*. Manhattan, KS: SASW/Comorian Studies, on diskette, 987,000 bytes; 10,000 entries.

Ottenheimer, Harriet Joseph, and Martin Ottenheimer. 1976. The classification of the languages of the Comoro Islands. *Anthropological Linguistics* 18(9): 408–415.

Payton, Walter. [1613] 1905. A journall of all principall matters passed in the twelfth voyage to the East-India . . . In Samuel Purchas (ed.), *Hakluytus Posthumus or Purchas his Pilgrimes* (Vol. 4). Glasgow: James Maclehose and Sons.

Peters, William. [1842–1848] 1856. In W. H. J. Bleek. *The languages of Mosambique: Vocabularies of the dialects of Lourenzo Marques, Inhambane, Sofala, Tette, Sena, Quellimane, Mosambique, Cape Delgado, Anjoane, the Maravi, Mudsau, etc., drawn from the manuscripts of Dr. Wm. Peters. M. Berl. Acad., and from other materials, by Dr. Wm. H. J. Bleek, Member of the German Oriental Society*. London: Harrison and Sons.

Pike, Kenneth L. 1947. *Phonemics: A technique for reducing languages to writing*. Ann Arbor: University of Michigan Press.

Powers, Willam K. 1990. Comment on the politics of orthography. *American Anthropologist* 92: 496–497.

Roe, Sir Thomas. [1615] 1905. Observations collected out of the journal of Sir Thomas Roe, Knight, Lord Embassadour from His Majestie of Great Britaine . . . Occurrents and Observations. In Samuel Purchas (ed.), *Hakluytus Posthumus or Purchas his Pilgrimes* (Vol. 4). Glasgow: James Maclehose and Sons.

Sacleux, Ch. 1909. *Grammaire des dialects swahilis*. Paris. Procure des PP. du Saint-Esprit.

———. 1939/41. *Dictionnaire swahili-français*. Vols. 1 & 2 (Travaux et mémoires de l'Institut d'Ethnologie 36–37). Paris: Musée de l'Homme.

———. 1949. *Dictionnaire français-swahili* (Travaux et mémoires de l'Institut d'Ethnologie 54). Paris: Musée de l'Homme.

Steere, E. [1869] 1920. *Short specimens of the vocabularies of three unpublished African languages*. London. In M. Heepe, Die Komorendialekte Ngadidja, Nzwani, und Mwali. *Abhanlungen des Hamburgischen Kolonialinstituts* 23:1–166.

Struck, B. 1909. An unpublished vocabulary of the Comoro language. *African Society Journal* 8:412–421.

Tabouret-Keller, Andrée, Robert B. Le Page, Penelope Gardner-Chloros, and Gabrielle Varro, eds. 1997. *Vernacular literacy: A re-evaluation*. Oxford Studies in Anthropological Linguistics. Oxford: Clarendon Press.

◈ WRITING/DISCUSSION EXERCISES

7.1   Read Ottenheimer's "Spelling Shinzwani . . ." Write a short summary of the article focusing on how different kinds of spelling systems can convey information about a person. Discuss your conclusions with your classmates. Compare your ideas about spelling and identity with your classmates. What differences and similarities do you notice?

7.2   Tape-record a few minutes of your own speech. Try taping part of a conversation with a friend in order to get the most natural and informal sounding pronunciations. Then listen to it and try to transcribe it as accurately as you can. Note the differences between how the words look on the page if you spell everything "just as it sounds" as opposed to using "correct spelling."

◈ PRACTICE WITH LANGUAGES

7.1. Japanese

The Japanese language can be written in several different ways. One method (kanji) is based on characters borrowed from the Chinese writing system. Another method (romaji) uses letters from the roman alphabet. Yet another writing system, the katakana syllabary, uses symbols to represent consonant-plus-vowel sequences. See the accompanying textbook for a full description of syllabaries. The chart below is a partial list of the symbols that make up the katakana syllabary of Japanese. Study the symbols and their pronunciations, and then answer questions a through e.

1	カ /ka/	キ /ki/	ク /ku/	ケ /ke/	コ /ko/
2	サ /sa/	シ /ʃi/	ス /su/	セ /se/	ソ /so/
3	タ /ta/	チ /tʃi/	ツ /tsu/	テ /te/	ト /to/
4	ナ /na/	ニ /ni/	ヌ /nu/	ネ /ne/	ノ /no/
5	ハ /ha/	ヒ /hi/	フ /fu/	ヘ /he/	ホ /ho/
6	マ /ma/	ミ /mi/	ム /mu/	メ /me/	モ /mo/

a. Consider the following examples:

   1 ガ /ga/
   2 ギ /gi/
   3 グ /gu/
   4 ゴ /go/

What important role does the diacritic play?

b. Based on your answer to question a, transcribe these symbols:

   1 ザ / /
   2 ヂ / /
   3 ゼ / /
   4 ド / /

c. Would it make sense for the diacritic ˚ to be added to any of the following symbols: ニ, ノ, マ, ム? Why or why not?

d. The diacritic ˚ indicates a voiced bilabial stop when associated with the symbols in row 5. For example, バ /ba/. Use this information to transcribe the following symbols:

   1 ビ / /
   2 ブ / /
   3 ベ / /
   4 ボ / /

e. The diacritic ° is combined with one of the above sets of symbols to create /pa/, /pi/, /pu/, /pe/, and /po/.

Write the katakana symbols that represent the following sound combinations. Choose just one set of basic symbols from the chart at the beginning of this exercise. Be sure to write the symbol ° to the upper right of each basic symbol.

1. _____ /pa/

2. _____ /pi/

3. _____ /pu/

4. _____ /pe/

5. _____ /po/

Explain, in phonetic terms, why you chose the symbols you did.

WEB EXERCISES

7.1 Follow the links on the companion website to the different sites where writing systems are presented and described. Use what you have learned in this chapter to recognize and analyze the graphemes of different writing systems. How long do you think it would take you to become literate in any of these scripts? How would reading this chapter have speeded up the process?

7.2   Follow the links on the companion website to the descriptions of the Pioneer Project and the symbolism on the plaque that was sent into space. Comment on how well you might be able to interpret the message on the plaque.

7.3   Search the InfoTrac database for articles about writing and literacy.

7.4   Search the InfoTrac database for articles about the ethnography of reading.

7.5   Search the InfoTrac database for articles about how writing in dialect reflects and re-inforces stereotypes.

◈ GUIDED PROJECTS

Language Creating

If your instructor has assigned this project, and you wish to do so, then this is the time to develop a writing system for your language. Your instructor will be your guide here, providing details as you need them. Hand in two copies of your group's work. Be sure to include your group's name, as well as the names of all of the individuals present who contributed to the day's work.

Conversation Partnering

If your instructor has assigned this project, you may be asked to compare and analyze similarities and differences in writing systems between you and your conversation partner. Your instructor will provide more details on how to do this.

CHAPTER 8

How (and When) Is Language Possible?

Note: Your instructor will indicate which readings, exercises, and/or projects you should do.

✳ READING

8.0 "Shintiri: The Secret Language of the Comoro Islands"
by Harriet Joseph Ottenheimer, with Davi and
Afan Ottenheimer

Harriet Ottenheimer's "Shintiri: The Secret Language of the Comoro Islands" could not have been written without the aid of her two sons. They were the ones who unlocked the secrets of Shintiri during a summer visit to the Comoros with their parents. At the time they were eleven and twelve years old and knew almost no Shinzwani. Ottenheimer wrote this article just a few years later, when her children were in high school, including them as co-authors to honor their role in gaining access to the secret play language of Comorian children.

This paper discusses the social and linguistic aspects of Shintiri, a secret play language (Sherzer 1976) or "ludling" (Laycock 1972:62) used by children in the Comoro Islands. The Comoro Archipelago, four islands in the Western Indian Ocean, lies at the northern end of the Mozambique Channel, almost exactly halfway between Madagascar and the east coast of Africa. Strategically located along ancient trading routes, the inhabitants of the Comoros have been exposed to a wide range of cultural and linguistic influences through the centuries (M. Ottenheimer 1976, 1984).

The indigenous languages of the Comoro Islands belong to the Bantu family of languages. Islanders refer to these languages by prefixing the class-marker, /shi-/ (or, in one case, the variant, /hi-/) to the name of each island. Thus, on the island of *Nzwani* one speaks *Shinzwani*, on the island of *Mwali* one speaks *Shimwali*, on the island of *Maori* one speaks *Shimaori* and on the island of *Ngazidja* one speaks *Shingazidja* or, alternatively, *Hingazidja*. The four islands are referred to collectively as *masiwa* (islands) and the word, *shimasiwa* is used to refer to all four languages collectively (H. and M. Ottenheimer 1976; H. Ottenheimer 1984)

In 1967–68, my husband Martin and I lived in the Comoro Islands as ethnographic field researchers. During our stay we collected samples of all four of the indigenous languages and became fluent in one of them, Shinzwani. There was a fifth language, however, which consistently eluded us. Try as we might, we could not find a speaker of the mysterious *Shintiri*.

Shintiri, we were told, was a language used by very few people. Repeatedly we were promised that a speaker of Shintiri would be found who would agree to teach us a few

Source: "Shintiri: The Secret Language of the Comoro Islands," by Harriet Joseph Ottenheimer, with Davi and Afan Ottenheimer, *Papers from the 20th Mid-America Linguistics Conference*, ed. James L. Armagost, pp. 181–188 (Kansas State University, 1985). Copyright 1985 Harriet Ottenheimer. Used by permission.

words. But this never came to pass. Eventually we were let in on at least a part of the mystery: Shintiri was a form of speech disguise, something like American Pig Latin. Jokes were made concerning the speakers of Shintiri: If the speakers of *Shinzwani* were *Wanzwani*, then were the speakers of *Shintiri* to be called *Wantiri*? And just where was the island of *Ntiri*? In spite of being let in on the jokes, however, we were never let in on the language.

Fourteen years later, in 1982, we returned to the Comoro Islands along with our two children who were, at the time, aged eleven and twelve. To ease their adjustment to a new language and a new culture, we prepared them by teaching them some basic aspects of Shinzwani along with some simple greetings and phrases. We provided them with notebooks and pens and asked them to document as much as they could about the construction and use of toys in the islands (H., A., and D. Ottenheimer, 1984).

The benefits of this approach to bringing children into the field proved to be even more than we expected. Not only did the boys adjust rapidly to their new surroundings, they also developed a greater understanding of the ethnographic research that their parents were engaged in. As trained "junior ethnographers" the boys collected information on palm-leaf pinwheels, sardine can whistles, sewing-spool cars, and many other toys. They learned to play a variety of games as well, and *Shintiri* turned out to be one of them! Imagine my surprise at walking into a room and finding a group of children teaching my own children to modify the little Shinzwani they had learned into some strange new set of sound patterns!

Was it the sociolinguistic constraints which had made it impossible for the parents to have learned Shintiri while allowing the children access to this mysterious language? Was Shintiri a pastime for children, and not for adults—even young adults such as we had been fifteen years earlier?

Comparative evidence appears to support this interpretation. While there are forms of disguised speech which are used by adult groups (such as thieves' cants and argots), play languages in which speech is disguised are usually considered the special preserve of children and adolescents (Burling 1970, Sherzer 1976, Kirshenblatt-Gimblett 1976). Some play languages are even considered to be more narrowly limited in use, for example, *Ngawani* used mainly by the sons of Zande princes in the Sudan. E. E. Evans-Pritchard notes, "Commoners knew what it was, their own language spoken backwards, and I suppose that had they tried to listen to it with care they could soon have followed it easily. They regarded it, however, as a game of princes' sons and one of their little jokes at the expense of themselves of which it was wiser and more dignified to take no notice" (Evans-Pritchard 1954:185). Even play languages that are widely known, such as *Baliktad*, spoken in the Philippines, are primarily children's languages. According to Harold Conklin, "although the use of *baliktad* is not restricted to any age, sex or social group, it is particularly popular among adolescents and unmarried teenagers" (Conklin 1956:139).

An example of a play language closer to the Comoros is *Kinyume* which, according to J. C. Trevor, "is said to be confined to women and children" among Swahili speakers in coastal Tanzania (Trevor 1955:96). Trevor reported having met one Comoro Islander who was "acquainted with it from childhood" and commented further that men appeared "rather abashed when asked if it was familiar to them" (Trevor 1955:96). Perhaps Trevor's experience with Kinyume is parallel to our own initial experience with Shintiri—for it was men who had informed us of the existence of Shintiri and who had joked about its speakers, while never actually producing either speakers or examples. The group of children that taught our children Shintiri consisted of girls between the ages of eight and fifteen years old. This is not to say that boys do not use Shintiri at all, but rather, that we had never observed boys, men, or indeed even adult women speaking or playing with Shintiri. It seems clear, therefore, that Shintiri had not been considered appropriate behavior either for us (as young adults) or for our adult informants back in 1967–68.

While play languages in general can be seen to function as social group markers, they are also of potential importance from the formal linguistic point of view. Play languages are generally rule-based derivations from conventional languages. As such they can be used to elucidate the structure of the conventional languages on which they are based.

Conklin used *Baliktad* to test "specific hypotheses concerning the combinatorial structure of Tagalog" (Conklin 1956). Campbell used *Jerigonza* as external evidence for Kekchi phonological rules (Campbell 1974). Play languages also provide unique windows into the ethnolinguistic intuition of their speakers. Sherzer used play languages in Cuna to gain valuable insights into native speakers' linguistic models (Sherzer 1976). Play languages play a valuable role in language learning. As children experiment with the underlying structures of their language they develop "productive competence in the word-internal, morphological features" of their language (Sanches and Kirshenblatt-Gimblett 1976:77).

All play languages make use of at least one of the four basic mechanisms of linguistic manipulation proposed by Mary Haas (1976): addition, subtraction, reversal, and substitution. Some combine several "rules" into a single "language" leading to rather complex constructions. Shintiri relies entirely on addition. It works as follows:

1. identify the first syllable of the word. In Shinzwani this is normally a CV
2. add the sound /-g-/ immediately following the Vowel of the syllable
3. repeat the Vowel of the syllable after the /-g-/
4. go on to the next syllable and repeat the entire process. Continue until every syllable has been treated

Thus, nikutsaha mazhi (I want water) becomes:

nigikugutsagahaga magazhigi

Note that the affricate, /-ts-/, is treated as a single segment. Other clusters that are treated as single segments are, /-dz-, -sh-, -zh-, -tr-, -dr-/ and the entire range of prenasalized consonants, /mp-, -mb-, -nt-, -nd-, -ntr-, ndr-, -nk-/ and /-ng/.

A final consonant is always given a vowel in Shintiri (and occasionally in Shinzwani as well). The one we heard most often was /-i-/, as in

Sharon   shagarogonigi

Double vowels are treated as if each vowel belongs to a separate syllable and occasionally consonants are invented for them as in,

bua   bugu(w)aga

or

waili   waga(y)igiligi

Particularly revealing is the treatment of foreign consonant clusters. These are generally separated into the smallest familiar segments, as in

Martin   magarigitiginigi

Note that both the medial /-r-/ and the final /-n-/ have vowels added to them.

Other play languages make use of the same kinds of manipulations. Although there may not be enough examples for a thorough comparative-historical analysis I will mention them here, nonetheless. Jerigonza, previously mentioned, is said to be originally a Spanish game, but it is reportedly used by Kekchi speakers in Guatemala. There are two versions of this play language, one using /p/ and one using /f/ (Campbell 1974:276). Edmonson (1971) has reported five different Spanish play languages. None of them is called Jerigonza but one of them, *Cifra,* found in New Mexico, follows the same pattern as Shintiri, using /f/ for the consonant (1971:209). Other play languages using /p/ or /f/ are: Rumanian *Pasareste* ("bird language"), which uses /p/ (Edmonson 1971:208), two different Indonesian play languages, one of which uses /p/ and the other of which uses /f/ (Sadtono 1971; Sherzer 1976:27), and several Russian play languages of which it is said that different consonants could be used on different days of the week, including /p/, /k/ and /r/ (Zim 1948:112). Both the Russian and the Indonesian examples differ slightly from Shintiri in that final consonants are not given vowels. The Russian example differs further in treating double vowels as single segments. /k/ is used as the consonant in Japanese (Burling

1970:136) and in Greek *Korakistika* or "crow language" (Edmonson 1971:208). One of the five different Cuna play languages described by Sherzer uses /r/ (Sherzer 1976:23), a Magyar play language inserts /v/ (but does not add vowels to final consonants) (Edmonson 1971:208), a Polish play language uses /nw/ (Edmonson 1971:208), and an American Pig Latin reported in California uses /lf/ (Cheney 1953:16–18). A German play language called *B Language* appears similar to Shintiri in that it repeats each syllable of a word, substituting /b/ for the first consonant in the repeated form (Schwartz 1982:25–27). Only one play language uses the /g/ of Shintiri. It is *Ziph*, a play language reported in England in the 1790s, and it appears to be identical to Shintiri (Schwartz 1982:41–43). All that is now known about Ziph is that it was taught to the English writer Thomas De Quincey by a doctor during a childhood illness. There was considerable contact between England and the Comoro Islands during this time period but any direct historical relationship between Ziph and Shintiri must remain a matter for speculation.

Perhaps it is because play languages are regarded as children's games that they have received so little scholarly attention. Perhaps, instead, it is because there are sociolinguistic barriers preventing scholars from obtaining information on these secret play languages. Whatever the reason, only a handful of folklorists, anthropologists and linguists have focused their attention on this important but elusive aspect of language use. Certainly more scholars must take an active interest in these creative linguistic games for our understanding of language in general to be complete. It also seems clear that more scholars should recognize the contributions that their children can make in this regard to research. Encouraging children to participate in field research is not a form of child-labor. Rather it is a means of recognizing the unique role that those children are already in as part of a family research team. Not only can such an approach ease their adjustment to a potentially difficult situation, it can also provide access to data which would otherwise be either unobtainable or overlooked.

Shintiri provided a way for Afan and Davi to enter into the child's world in the Comoros. They didn't ask to learn Shintiri. They probably didn't even know it existed until they were taught it. In any case, a small group of girls was sufficiently concerned to take the time to initiate them into the mysteries of this secret play language, making certain that they could at least change their names into Shintiri. Of course it is possible that the sociolinguistic barriers Martin and I had encountered in the 1960s had simply been removed by the 1980s—or perhaps modified.

Perhaps any one of us could have learned Shintiri in 1982, had we just asked. The point is that although none of us asked, some of us were taught. I am convinced, however, that without Afan and Davi we would never have learned Shintiri at all.

REFERENCES

Burling, Robbins. 1970. *Man's Many Voices.* New York: Holt, Rinehart and Winston.

Campbell, Lyle. 1974. Theoretical Implications of Kekchi Phonology. *International Journal of American Linguistics* 40(4) Part 1:269–278.

Cheney, William Murray. 1953. *A Pamphlet on the Four Basic Dialects of Pig Latin.* Los Angeles, CA.

Conklin, Harold. 1956. Tagalog Speech Disguise. *Language* 32:136–139.

Edmonson, Munro. 1971. *Lore: An Introduction to the Science of Folklore and Literature.* New York: Holt, Rinehart and Winston.

Evans-Pritchard, E. E. 1954. A Zande Slang Language. *Man* 54:289.

Haas, Mary R. 1967. Taxonomy of Disguised Speech. Paper presented to the Linguistic Society of America.

Kirshenblatt-Gimblett, Barbara. 1976. *Speech Play: Research and Resources for Studying Linguistic Creativity.* Philadelphia: University of Pennsylvania Press.

Laycock, D. 1972. Towards a Typology of Ludlings, or Play-Languages. *Linguistic Communications, Working Papers of the Linguistic Society of Australia* 6:61–113. Clayton, Victoria: Monash University.

Masson, David (ed.). 1889–1890. *The Collected Writings of Thomas De Quincey, New Edition, Vol. I (Autobiography)*. Edinburgh, Scotland: Adam and Charles Black.

Ottenheimer, Harriet. 1984. A Shinzwani-English Dictionary for the Comoro Islands. Papers of the Annual Meeting of the African Studies Association. Los Angeles: Crossroads Press.

Ottenheimer, Harriet, Afan and Davi. 1984. The Family as an Ethnographic Team. Paper presented to the Central States Anthropological Society. Lincoln, NE.

Ottenheimer, Harriet and Martin. 1976. The Classification of the Languages of the Comoro Islands. *Anthropological Linguistics* December: 408–415.

Ottenheimer, Martin. 1976. Multiethnicity and Trade in the Western Indian Ocean Area. In W. Arens, ed., *A Century of Change in Eastern Africa*. The Hague: Mouton.

———. 1984. *Marriage in Domoni: Husbands and Wives in an Indian Ocean Community*. Prospect Heights, IL: Waveland Press.

Sadtono, E. 1971. Language Games in Javanese. In J. L. Sherzer, L. Foley, Sister C. Johnson, N. A. Johnson, A. Palakornkul, and E. Sadtono, *A Collection of Linguistic Games (Penn-Texas Working Papers in Sociolinguistics 2)*. Austin: University of Texas, pp. 32–38.

Sanches, Mary, and Barbara Kirshenblatt-Gimblett. 1976. Children's Traditional Speech Play and Child Language. In Barbara Kirshenblatt-Gimblett, ed., *Speech Play: Research and Resources for Studying Linguistic Creativity*. Philadelphia: University of Pennsylvania Press, pp. 19–36.

Schwartz, Alvin. 1982. *The Cat's Elbow and Other Secret Languages*. New York: Farrar Straus Giroux.

Sherzer, Joel. 1976. Play Languages: Implications for (Socio)Linguistics. In Barbara Kirshenblatt-Gimblett, ed., *Speech Play: Research and Resources for Studying Linguistic Creativity*. Philadelphia: University of Pennsylvania Press.

Trevor, J. C. 1955. Backwards Languages in Africa. *Man* 55:111.

Zim, Herbert S. 1948. *Codes and Secret Writing*. New York: William Morrow and Company.

◈ WRITING/DISCUSSION EXERCISES

8.1 Read Ottenheimer's "Shintiri." Write a short summary of the article focusing on how children's play languages can provide insight into the beginnings of language. How does Pig Latin make use of Hockett's design feature of "duality of patterning"? Be prepared to discuss Pig Latin and duality of patterning with your classmates.

8.2   If you know or have ever used a variety of Pig Latin in your own language, take some time to analyze the way that it works. How does it compare to Shintiri? Is it syllable-based? Or is there some other basis? See if you can write out the rules for producing hidden words in your variety of Pig Latin. Compare your variety of Pig Latin, and its rules, with any that your classmates have. Are there similarities? differences? What do the similarities and differences suggest to you about Pig Latin in general? About language in general?

8.3   There is a popular movement which encourages parents to teach their babies to sign as early as possible. Proponents of this movement suggest that babies are able to learn and communicate in sign language well before they are able to communicate using spoken words. If you know anyone who has a young infant, ask them if they have heard of this, and if so whether they have experimented with it. What do you think success with teaching babies to sign before speaking suggests about the emergence of human language?

◈ WEB EXERCISES

8.1   Go to the companion website and follow the links about some of the ape-language experiments. Write a short essay about these experiments. With reference to Hockett's design features of language, does it seem to you that the experiments are demonstrating language use in apes? Which features seem present? Which features seem to be missing? How can you tell?

8.2   Go to the companion website and follow the links to some of the research being done on language and brains. Explore the various diagrams on those sites and then make a list of functions which appear to map to the different sides of the brain. Do any of the sites pay attention to signed as well as spoken language? Why do you think they include or exclude sign language? What are the implications of excluding sign language from brain-language research?

8.3 Go to the companion website and follow the links to discussions about the development of the human capacity for language. Write a short essay summarizing the different positions on this subject: to what extent do scholars think that language developed from gestures? to what extent do they think that language developed directly from primate calls? to what extent do they pay attention to the role of children in the emergence of human language?

8.4 Go to the companion website and follow the link to Kenneth Pike's autobiographical narrative. Read the section in which he discusses experimenting with his daughter's intonation patterns. Comment on what this tells you about language learning in social settings.

8.5   Search the InfoTrac database for articles about the origins of language.

8.6   Search the InfoTrac database for articles about ape-language experiments.

8.7   Search the InfoTrac database for articles about language and the brain.

GUIDED PROJECTS

Language Creating

If you are creating a language, you may want to design a "Pig Latin" for it.

Conversation Partnering

If your instructor has assigned this project, you may be asked to check with your conversation partner to see if he or she knows of a "Pig Latin" or secret play language in his or her language. If so, then see if you can learn it. What are the rules that you need to know to produce Pig Latin words in your conversation partner's language? How are these rules similar to and different from any Pig Latin that you are already familiar with from your own language?

CHAPTER 9

Change and Choice

Note: Your instructor will indicate which readings, exercises, and/or projects you should do.

READING

9.0 "English as an Official Language: The Nebraska Experience" by Robert S. Haller

Robert Haller's "English as an Official Language" provides chilling insight into the history of the English Only movement. It makes it clear that nativist movements have been around for a long time, and it suggests that one reason many contemporary Nebraskans are not bilingual is due to the linguistic choices that their grandparents and great-grandparents made in the early part of the 1900s. Faced with the disapproval of their Anglo neighbors, and the passage of a law requiring them to abandon their ancestral languages, many chose to raise their children as monolinguals. It also helps to provide insight into the ways in which the United States continues to stress its status as a monolingual country.

This paper is intended to be timely; there is currently a move to have English declared the official language of this country, and the arguments for such a constitutional amendment are being carried on as if there were no relevant history and precedent. The issue is one concerning which linguists can be helpful and with regard to which they are interested parties. Nebraska has currently in the Bill of Rights of its Constitution (Appendix 3) a provision making English the official language of the state. This provision got there by vote of the people in 1920, in the midst of a reaction to immigration and an emphasis on Americanism, both brought to a head by World War I. The general story of such policies in Nebraska and other states has been told before (Ferguson/Heath 1980; Leibowitz 1976). It is my object in this paper to look at aspects of the public and forensic arguments in order to highlight certain assumptions about language which were influential in creating public support for the measure. I will concentrate on two of these: the alleged consequences of thinking in a foreign language; and the effects of learning foreign languages at an early age. Linguists know a great deal about these issues. Insofar as they are still live issues, linguists can contribute to the debate about English as an official language.

But first, a brief outline of the essential events. In 1919, the so-called Simon Language Bill (Appendix 1) was passed by the Nebraska Legislature. On December 26 of that year, the Supreme Court of Nebraska found the act constitutional in answering a suit by the Nebraska District, Evangelical Lutheran Church, asking for a declaratory judgment. A Constitutional Convention met in the years 1919–20. It considered and passed a provision in the Bill of Rights, rejecting the stronger original proposal (Appendix 2), making English the official language of the expressed purpose of reinforcing the Simon Language Bill. The

Source: Robert S. Haller, "English as an Official Language: The Nebraska Experience," *Papers from the 20th Mid-America Linguistics Conference,* ed. James L. Armagost (Kansas State University, 1985).

voters of the state adopted this provision in 1920. In May of that year Robert T. Meyer was arrested and convicted of teaching German under the Simon Law. In 1921, the Legislature strengthened the 1919 law by incorporating the language of the constitutional provision and by trying to assure that the law did not violate religious liberty (Appendix 4). In 1922, the Nebraska Supreme Court confirmed the constitutionality of the new law by upholding (February 1922) Meyer's conviction and in rejecting another suit brought by the Lutherans asking for a declaratory judgment on the constitutionality of the new law. But on further appeal, the U.S. Supreme Court (Meyer vs. Nebraska; Argued Feb. 23 1923; Decided June 4 1923), in a landmark decision, found the law unconstitutional and overturned Meyer's conviction, at the same time reversing convictions under similar laws in Iowa and Ohio. But the Supreme Court decision did not deny the constitutionality of declaring English the official language of the state, nor of providing that it be the language of instruction in schools. Thus the provision remains in the Nebraska Constitution.

The reasoning behind the Simon Language Bill was well explained by Judge Letton in upholding its constitutionality in the Nebraska Supreme Court when he pointed to that "condition in the body politic" whose "evil consequences" were exposed by the draft law of 1917. It was well known that "thousands of men born in this country" had been taught in the language of their parents, and therefore could not "read, write or speak" English, being thus rendered unable to "understand words of command given in English." But worse than that,

> it was also demonstrated that there were local foci of alien enemy sentiment, and that, where such instances occurred, the education given by private or parochial schools in that community was usually found to be that which had been given mainly in a foreign language. (175 NW 533)

One could understand a concern with military communication and discipline. It may be possible also that knowledge of a foreign language allowed people to read materials in that language which encouraged disloyalty (although knowledge of German might also be used to possible advantage for the United States). What is more difficult to understand is the apparent assumption that *thinking* in a foreign language was inherently dangerous to the state. Judge Flansburg is explicit on the "baneful effects" which he calls "inimical to our own safety" of allowing children to be reared in their native tongue:

> It was to educate them so that they must always think in that language, and, as a consequence, naturally inculcate in them the ideas and sentiments foreign to the best interests of this country. (187 NW 102)

All of the debate in the Legislature and Constitutional Convention, and the decisions of the Nebraska Supreme Court upholding the language laws, appeals to this natural connection between a foreign language and foreign, alien thinking. Indeed, Americans seemed to believe that even talking in foreign languages [was] dangerous to the state. Walter Anderson, of Lancaster County, the introducer of the constitutional amendment, recalled, in a tolerant mood, that when he was draft executive of Nebraska, people

> were running to me with this and that and the other story of some old German talking over the telephone or passing the time of day on the street corner talking in German and saying that had to be stopped. (Proceedings 1297)

Anderson himself did not try to teach old dogs new tricks. But he did resolve to make sure that the children of these people would escape from this trap of a foreign language. As he phrased it,

> We want every child that grows up in America, no matter where his parents were born, no matter what sentiment they have in favor of the old homeland across the water, no matter how unpatriotic for that matter his parents may be, we want that child to have the English language, that is, the language of this country, for his language. (Proceedings 1296)

The natural correlate of this idea was that English was the only language in which *American* ideas could be expressed. Anderson, indeed, preferred to call it the American language, and used this term in his proposed amendment to the constitution. His subcommittee substituted *English* for *American;* but he, as Chair, inserted a [sic] after "English" in the wording he submitted to the Convention. In presenting the amendment, he explained that "the words are more or less immaterial" but that he himself preferred American, being "for one country, one language and one flag," all called American. Cooler heads prevailed. Mr. Wiltse pointed out from the floor that "there is no such thing as the American language unless we refer to the language of the American Indian" (Proceedings 954), and Judge Wall added that existing Federal and State requirements used the term "English" already. An amendment to reintroduce the substitution of "American" for "English" failed by only one vote. It would perhaps be useful in focusing the issue if the substitution had succeeded, for it embodies this Whorfian assumption that each ideology has its specific language in which it is expressed.

Indeed, all interested parties stressed the fact that English was the medium of American ideas. It was first of all, as Anderson declared, the language of the Declaration of Independence and the Constitutions of the country and state. It was thus, in general, as the explanation of the Proposed Amendments presented to the voters so aptly said, "the language in which the spirit of our institutions is expressed" (Amendments 5). Judge Letton in upholding the constitutionality of the Simon Language Law, appealed to the already existing provisions of the school law which required instruction "in American history and in civil government, both state and national, such as will give the pupils a thorough knowledge of the history of our country, its Constitution, and our form of government," and construed the Simon law as instrumental in promoting for "all children, whether of foreign born parents, or of native citizens," the state's legitimate object, which he described as

> *the upbuilding of an intelligent American citizenship, familiar with the principles and ideals upon which this government was founded, to imbue the alien child with the tradition of our past, to give him the knowledge of the lives of Washington, Franklin, Adams, Lincoln and other men who lived in accordance with such ideas, and to teach him love for his country, and hatred of dictatorship, whether by autocrats, by the proletariat, or by any man, or class of men. (175 NW 534)*

Although these arguments could be construed simply to say that it was easier to acquire American values in the English language, it is clear from the intensity of the insistence on this principle that supporters of the Simon Bill believed that the English or American language itself uniquely expressed the traditional attitudes of this country.

But Judge Letton and the other supporters of the principle were aware that promoting English was one thing, and forbidding foreign language instruction quite another. The latter might be seen as exceeding the limits on the state's power. In this context, Judge Letton ingeniously proposed that the forbidding of the teaching of foreign languages could be construed as freeing a pupil's study time for the learning—in English—of subjects essential to the building of citizenship. But the proposers of the Simon Bill and of the constitutional amendment wished to forbid the teaching of foreign languages until graduation from eighth grade because they well understood that in their earlier years children could more rapidly and thoroughly either maintain, or acquire, competence in a foreign language. The age, in other words, was deliberately set to assure, as far as possible, the eradication of bilingualism, the undermining of family ties in immigrant families, and the discouraging of foreign language acquisition on the part of English speakers. Judge Farnsburg observes, for instance, that the prohibition did not apply to the "so-called ancient or dead languages, not being, strictly speaking, foreign languages" (187 NW 928) but only to those languages which might actually be spoken in the community. It was granted that a few persons not belonging to the "foreign element of our population" might desire "to have their children instructed in a foreign language before the children have passed the eighth grade." But Judge Farnsburg maintained that the "individual rights" of these few "must yield to the general public benefit."

That it was only a small number of native English speakers who desired their children to receive earlier instruction in foreign languages is partly indicated by the existence of politicians like Senator Oleson, who boasted at the Constitutional Convention that he had stood, for "nearly twenty years . . . for taking out of the public schools of this state the teaching of all foreign languages" because he believed that this was a subject that ought not to be taught "at public expense" (Proceedings 960). Judge Letton, dissenting from Judge Farnsburg's opinion that the state could legitimately prohibit the teaching of foreign languages even outside of school hours (but concurring in the majority concerning the school hours themselves) made explicit the assumption behind that prohibition when he pointed out that "Educators agree that the period of early childhood is the time that the ability to speak or understand a foreign, or a classic, language is the most easily acquired." He thus insisted that the "legitimate object of the statute has been accomplished" when basic education is carried out in English, but would not exclude, beyond this, instruction at an early age in a foreign language.

The framers of the Simon Language Bill and of the Constitutional Provision, on the other hand, were more interested in weaning the children of foreigners away from parental instruction than in encouraging native children to acquire foreign languages. As Anderson himself said in offering his amendment,

> *You could paraphrase this by saying it is merely a declaration that every American Kiddie, no matter where his parents were born, has an absolute and inherent right to the American language as his first language, and that no person is going to pass any law that will interfere with that kiddie getting the American language first. (Proceedings 961)*

Not only did the proponents wish to drive a wedge between parent and child; they were trying to destroy ethnic communities as a political base. Again, quoting Anderson. He accused supporters of the "denatured" substitute for his proposal of wanting to go back and tell the man "who wanted to keep alive the old language and who wanted to keep little Italys and little Bohemias in the Constitution" that the law did not interfere with their desire; and he complained that "these old languages die hard," and that when he talked to "a German or to a Bohemian if there is such a hybrid any more" that man will begin to refer to "our language" and mean by that expression "the Bohemian or Slavonian or German or whatever he is talking about" (Proceedings 1297).

The knowledge of such intentions embarrassed the Nebraska Supreme Court which, in upholding the constitutionality of the Bill in a challenge from the Evangelical Lutheran Church, had to resort to hair-splitting. The Court insisted that the Legislature could not have intended to pass an unconstitutional law. Thus a proper interpretation of the law "had to focus, not on 'the words' of the particular measure," but to the "mischief which the Legislature was endeavoring to remedy" (175 NW 535). The U.S. Supreme Court was unwilling to ignore the plain language of the Bill, and declared it unconstitutional, asserting that "The protection of the Constitution extends to all, to those who speak other languages as well as to those born with English on the tongue," and appealing to the basic "privileges long recognized at common law as essential to the orderly pursuit of happiness by free men," including the right to "bring up children" and "worship God." Thus only Article 1, Section 27 of the Nebraska Constitution survives from this legislative and constitutional ferment. And Shepard's Nebraska Citations shows that this provision has not been referred to in any decision since its incorporation into the Constitution. Let me say here that I have in this paper ignored the arguments of the Simon Bill's opponents, which were generally intelligent, and appealed to a larger context of national policy and precedent. I have also ignored the good natured arguments of the advocates, and the thoughtful arguments of some of their allies. I should note here that not all advocates of English as an official language were as malicious or casuistical as those I have quoted. Justice Holmes, for instance, (with Mr. Justice Sutherland concurring) dissented from the Supreme Court decision in Meyer vs. Nebraska, explaining

> *I cannot bring my mind to believe that in some circumstances, and circumstances existing it is said in Nebraska, the statute might not be regarded as a reasonable or even necessary method of reaching the desired result. The part of the act with which we are concerned deals with the teaching of young children. Youth is the time when familiarity with a language is established and if there are sections in the State where a child would hear only Polish or French or German spoken at home I am not prepared to say that it is unreasonable to provide that in his early years he shall hear and speak only English at school. But if it is reasonable it is not an undue restriction of the liberty either of teacher or scholar. (43 Sup. Ct. 630)*

The current advocates of English as an official language may be just as well-meaning as Justice Holmes, and just as concerned for the welfare of youth growing up without the benefit of English. But I note that it is rarely the non-English speakers themselves who express this concern. It is probably counter to our national interest that we continue to believe that only English expresses American ideals, and that foreign language instruction is best put off until the high school years, when there is no danger of its being learned effectively. It is probably counter to our national interest that we discourage over most of the country and especially in Nebraska a public life carried on in languages other than English. Such a policy probably carries over unconsciously into our international life, where we seem to believe that foreigners need English more than we need their languages for the enhancement of international understanding in all its aspects. Some linguists have attempted to counter the Whorfianism of these language attitudes (e.g., Weinstein 1983:19–34) and to suggest that our language history should encourage us to consider its variety as a resource to be husbanded rather than as a danger to be eradicated (Ferguson/Heath 1980:6–20). I should hope that we could all join in the current controversy to assure that its outcome is sound.

Appendix 1
SIMON LANGUAGE BILL (1919) (175 NW 532–33)

An act relating to the teaching of foreign languages in the state of Nebraska.

Section 1. No person, individually or as a teacher, shall, in any private, denominational, parochial or public school, teach any subject to any person in any language than the English language.

Section 2. Languages, other than the English language, may be taught as languages only after a pupil shall have attained and successfully passed the eighth grade as evidenced by a certificate of graduation issued by the county superintendent of the county in which the child resides.

Section 3. Any person who violates any of the provisions of this act shall be deemed guilty of a misdemeanor and upon conviction, shall be subject to a fine of not less than twenty-five ($25) dollars, nor more than one hundred ($100) dollars or be confined in the county jail for a period not exceeding thirty days for each offense.

Appendix 2
PROCEEDINGS OF THE CONSTITUTIONAL CONVENTION 1919–20

Proposal #77. Walter R. Anderson. Relating to the right of the people to a common language.

The ability of the people to freely communicate with and understand each other is essential to a republican form of government, and a common language being therefore a necessity to the people of this state, the right of the people to such a common language shall never be denied or in any way impaired or abridged. To that end, the American language—the language of the Declaration of Independence, of the Federal Constitution and of this Constitution—is hereby declared to be such a common language and no other, and no person shall be taught in or taught any other language in any school, public or private, until such person shall have attained the age of 14 years and shall be able to understandingly read, write and speak such American language.

Appendix 3
CONSTITUTION OF THE STATE OF NEBRASKA (1983)
ARTICLE I—BILL OF RIGHTS

Section 27. The English language is hereby declared to be the official language of this state, and all official proceedings, records and publications shall be in such language, and the common school branches shall be taught in said language in public, private, denominational and parochial schools.

Appendix 4
REVISION, 1921
(THE NEBRASKA SCHOOL LAWS 1921:111–12)

An act to declare the English language the official language of this state, and to require all official proceedings, records and publications to be in such language and all school branches to be taught in said language in public, private, denominational and parochial schools; to prohibit discrimination against the use of the English language by social, religious or commercial organizations; to provide a penalty for a violation thereof; to repeal ch. 249 of the Session Laws of Nebraska for 1919.

Section 1. English, official language. (Same language as Art 1, Sect 27, Nebraska Constitution)

Section 2. Other languages, teaching forbidden.—No person, individually or as a teacher, shall, in any private, denominational, or parochial or public school, teach any subject to any person in any language other than the English language.

Section 3. Same, exceptions.—Languages other than the English language may be taught as languages only after a pupil shall have attained and successfully passed the eighth grade as evidenced by a certificate of graduation issued by the county superintendent of the county or the city superintendent of the city in which the child resides. Provided, that the provisions of this act shall not apply to schools held on Sunday or on some other day of the week which those having the care and custody of the pupils attending same conscientiously observe as the Sabbath, where the object and purpose of such school is the giving of religious instruction, but shall apply to all other schools and to schools held at all other times. Provided that nothing in this act shall prohibit any person from teaching his own children in his own home any foreign language.

Section 4. Unlawful to discriminate.—It shall be unlawful for any organization, whether social, religious or commercial, to prohibit, forbid or discriminate against the use of the English language in any meeting, school or proceeding, and for any officer, director, member or person in authority in any organization to pass, promulgate, connive at, publish, enforce or attempt to enforce any such prohibition or discrimination.

Section 5. Violation, penalty.—Any public official, teacher, instructor, or other person who shall violate any of the provisions of this act shall be deemed guilty of a misdemeanor and upon conviction thereof be fined in any sum not exceeding one hundred ($100.00) dollars or less than twenty-five ($25.00) dollars, or be imprisoned in the county jail for a period not exceeding thirty days for each offense.

REFERENCES

Constitution of the State of Nebraska. Edited and distributed by Allen J. Beermann, Secretary of State. 1983. Cited as Constitution.

Ferguson, F. A., and S. B. Heath, eds. 1980. *Language in the USA*. Cambridge: Cambridge University Press.

Leibowitz, Arnold H. 1976. Language and the law: The exercise of power through official designation of language. In *Language and Politics*, W. M. O'Barr and J. F. O'Barr, eds. The Hague: Mouton.

Meyer vs. State of Nebraska (1923). 43 Sup. Ct. 625–28g. 187 NW 100–5.

Proceedings of the Constitutional Convention 1919–20. Cited as Proceedings.

Nebraska District of Evangelical Lutheran Synod of Missouri, Ohio, and Other States et al. (St. Wenceslaus Church of Omaha et al., Interveners) v. McKelvie, Governor, et al. 175 NW 531–36.

Nebraska District of Evangelical Lutheran Synod of Missouri, Ohio, and Other States (Siefken et al., Interveners) v. McKelvie et al. 187 NW 927–30.

Proposed Amendments to the Constitution of the State of Nebraska as adopted by the Constitutional Convention 1919–20 with Explanatory Statements and Sample Ballot. 1920. Cited as Amendments.

Weinstein, Brian. 1983. *The Civic Tongue: Political Consequences of Language Choices*. New York and London: Longman.

 ## WRITING/DISCUSSION EXERCISES

9.1   Read Haller's "English as an Official Language." Write a short summary of the article focusing on the impact of English Only kinds of movements on language choice in the United States. Discuss this impact with your classmates. Do they agree with you or disagree with you?

9.2 Discuss the advantages and disadvantages of being monolingual in today's world. Compare your answers with those of your classmates. Take a poll in class and discuss the results.

9.3 Discuss the advantages and disadvantages of learning a second language in school or at home. Compare your answers with those of your classmates. Take a poll in class and discuss the results.

9.4   Make a list of words that are a part of your vocabulary that are not a part of your parents' vocabulary. What does this tell you about the rate at which language changes? Compare your results with those of your classmates. See if you can account for any differences in rates of language change among your peers.

 PRACTICE WITH LANGUAGES

9.1   Reconstructing Proto-Polynesian

Here are some words from four related contemporary Polynesian languages. Each numbered group of words is a set of cognates. An English gloss (approximate translation) is provided for each set of cognates:

	Maori	Hawai'ian	Samoan	Fijian	English gloss
1	pou	pou	pou	bou	post
2	tapu	kapu	tapu	tabu	forbidden
3	taŋi	kani	taŋi	taŋi	cry
4	takere	kaʔele	taʔele	takele	keel
5	hono	hono	fono	vono	stay, sit
6	marama	malama	malama	malama	light, moon, dawn
7	kaho	ʔaho	ʔaso	kaso	thatch

Step 1: Correspondence Sets
Use the cognate sets above to fill in the blanks in the table of correspondence sets below. Vowels go on lines A through E and consonants go on lines F through N. Some sets have been filled in for you, and the Maori column has been completely filled in. Your job is to find the sounds in each of the other languages that correspond with those Maori sounds. For example, an /a/ in Maori appears as an /a/ in Hawai'ian, an /a/ in Samoan, and an /a/ in Fijian. You can confirm this by looking at correspondence sets numbered 2, 3, 4, 6, and 7, so those numbers should appear on line A under the heading "Cognate set #." Likewise, the sounds that correspond to the Maori /p/ (correspondence set F) are /p/ in Hawai'ian, /p/ in Samoan, and /b/ in Fijian, which is confirmed by examining correspondence sets 1 and 2. Compare all of the words and fill in all of the blanks. Note that the cognate set numbers have been filled in for correspondence sets M and N. We will have more to say about this in step 2. You can ignore the "Reconstruction" column until we get to step 2.

	Maori	Hawai'ian	Samoan	Fijian	Cognate set #	Reconstruction
A	/a/	/a/	/a/	/a/	2,3,4,6,7	/*a/
B	/e/					
C	/i/					
D	/o/					
E	/u/					
F	/p/	/p/	/p/	/b/	1,2	/*p/
G	/t/					
H	/k/					
I	/r/					
J	/m/					
K	/n/					
L	/ŋ/					
M	/h/				5	
N	/h/	/h/	/s/	/s/	7	/*s/

Step 2: Reconstructing Protophonemes
Once you have all of the cognate sets filled in, it is time to attempt some reconstructions. Three sets have already been filled in, to get you started. Using these as a model, reconstruct protophonemes for the remaining sets. In most cases you can use the rule of "majority." For example, if all four contemporary languages show an /a/, then the most likely reconstruction is /*a/. If a majority of the contemporary languages show the same sound, it is fairly safe to use that sound for your reconstruction. Note that an asterisk designates a reconstruction; /*a/, /*p/, and /*s/ are reconstructions in this example.

Where there is no clear majority you will have more trouble. Here you will need to pay attention to two other principles of reconstruction. One is that /*h/ is almost never reconstructed. This leads us to choose /*s/ for correspondence set N. The other is that the overall set of protophonemes should appear "balanced" on a standard phonetic chart. This means that you will have to go back and forth between steps 2 and 3 before you can complete your reconstructions with confidence.

Step 3: Charting the Protophonemes

Arrange all of the reconstructed protophonemes into standard phonetic chart format. Make one chart for all of the protoconsonants and another chart for all of the proto-vowels. Examine your charts for "balance" (also called "pattern congruity"). For example, if you have /*p/, /*t/, and /*k/ for voiceless stops, then your other sounds (voiced stops, fricatives, nasals, and so on) should occupy the same (or similar) columns (bilabial, alveolar, and velar in this case) on your phonetic chart. If either one of your charts seems "out of balance" in any way, go back to step 2 and adjust your reconstructions to create better balance.

Step 4: Developing Rules

Now you should generate some "rules" to show how the protophonemes could have evolved into their contemporary variants. For example, in correspondence set F you can see that /*p/ remained the same in Maori, Hawai'ian, and Samoan; but in Fijian it changed over time so that now it is pronounced /b/. You can write this as /*p/ → /b/, which means that proto /*p/ evolves into /b/. Note that this rule is only listed in the Fijian column. Wherever there is a change you should create a rule to describe it. List each rule in the appropriate column below. Some rules may have to be listed under more than one language.

Maori changes	Hawai'an changes	Samoan changes	Fijian changes
			/*p/ → /b/

Extra Credit: Are there any general phonetic processes that you can identify in any of the rules you have created? Can you describe these processes? Can you write a set of rules that shows these processes?

Step 5: Protowords

Use your protophonemes to create protowords for each word on the list. These will show what the original words might have sounded like in the ancestral Protopolynesian language. Don't forget to use asterisks to indicate that these are reconstructions.

1. post
2. forbidden
3. cry
4. keel
5. stay, sit
6. light, moon, dawn
7. thatch

WEB EXERCISES

9.1 Go to the companion website and follow the links to sites discussing language change. In particular, look at some examples of change in your own language. What are some of the pressures for change that your language has encountered throughout history? What are some contemporary pressures for change in your language?

9.2 Go to the companion website and follow the links to some of the research on language variation over space. In particular, look for sites that reflect research being done on your primary language. What dialects are there in your language? What are the geographical boundaries of those dialects? What are the social markers of those dialects? How many of those dialects are you familiar with?

9.3   Go to the companion website and follow the links to discussions of the English Only movement. Write a short essay about the issues involved. Who is arguing in favor of making the United States a monolingual country? Who is arguing against? What are the advantages? What are the disadvantages? Can you think of other countries that are completely monolingual? Are they completely unified politically and socially? Why does a single language not guarantee political unity?

9.4   Go to the companion website and follow the links to the official page of the Canadian Government. Read about the language policies adopted by Canada. What are the advantages of maintaining bilingualism in Canada? What are the disadvantages? What is Canada doing to maintain the political unity of its country in spite of the fact that it is officially bilingual?

9.5   Search the InfoTrac database for articles about language change over time.

9.6   Search the InfoTrac database for articles about how language varies over geographical and social space.

9.7   Search the InfoTrac database for articles about Ebonics.

9.8   Search the InfoTrac database for articles about pidgin and Creole languages.

◈ GUIDED PROJECTS

Language Creating

If you are creating a language, you may want to send a representative from your group to contact the speakers of a "different" group in your class. Borrow a word or two from that group's language. Bring those words "home" to your own language-creating group and teach it to the other members of your group. Examine the phonological system of your language and assess how you might pronounce these new words. Do you suppose you could learn to pronounce these new words easily? What are the chances that the new words would add a new sound to your overall sound system? What other effects might the new words have on your language?

Conversation Partnering

If your instructor has assigned this project, you may be asked to research the linguistic family trees of your two languages. How closely related do your two languages appear to be in linguistic terms? How distant? Are they members of the same language family? different language families but the same macro-family? If speakers of your two languages came into contact in a long-term trading situation, what kind of pidgin language do you think they might create?

CHAPTER 10

Doing Linguistic Anthropology

Note: Your instructor will indicate which readings, exercises, and/or projects you should do.

❋ READING

10.0 "Mock Spanish: A Site for the Indexical Reproduction
of Racism in American English" by Jane H. Hill

> Jane Hill's "Mock Spanish: A Site for the Indexical Reproduction of Racism in American English" explores important questions regarding how the language we use can express racist ideas at a deeply unconscious level. Most Anglo speakers are not consciously aware of the implications of the specific phrases and mispronunciations that Hill points out; instead they find them to be "charming" or "funny." Yet Hill's analysis is an important one and it should make us realize how easily our language can convey ideas and attitudes. Hill's article challenges you to think about your language. It also challenges you to make use of all of the linguistic anthropology skills you have learned, from analyzing phonology, morphology, and syntax to understanding language in action and questions of change and choice. You will probably find yourself using knowledge gained from every other chapter of our text as you read Hill's article. Although the article is no longer online, you can view the complete set of slides by going to the companion website for this book and following the appropriate link.

Introduction

I was first drawn to the study of "Mock Spanish"[1] by a puzzle. In the southwestern United States, English speakers of "Anglo"[2] ethnic affiliation make considerable use of Spanish in casual speech, in spite of the fact that the great majority of them are utterly monolingual in English under most definitions. However, these monolinguals both produce Spanish and consume it, especially in the form of Mock Spanish humor. Mock Spanish has, I believe, intensified during precisely the same period when opposition to the use of Spanish by its native speakers has grown, reaching its peak in the passage of "Official English" statutes in several states during the last decade.[3]

As I began to explore this question, I realized that I had also engaged a larger one: In a society where for at least the last 20 years to be called a "racist" is a dire insult, and where opinion leaders almost universally concur that "racism" is unacceptable, how is racism continually reproduced? For virulent racism unquestionably persists in the United States. People of color feel it intensely in almost every dimension of their lives. Studies by researchers of every political persuasion continue to show substantial gaps between the several racialized groups and so-called "whites" on every quantifiable dimension of economic prosperity, educational success, and health (including both infant mortality and life expectancy). I argue here that everyday talk, of a type that is almost never characterized (at least by Anglos) as "racist," is one of the most important sites for the covert reproduction of this racism. "Mock Spanish," the topic of this paper, is one example of such a site.

Source: Jane H. Hill, "Mock Spanish: A Site for the Indexical Reproduction of Racism in American English," *Language & Culture: Symposium* 2 (1995). © Jane H. Hill. Used by permission.

"Mock Spanish" exemplifies a strategy of dominant groups that I have called, following Raymond Williams (1977), "incorporation" (Hill 1995). By "incorporation" members of dominant groups expropriate desirable resources, both material and symbolic, from subordinate groups. Through incorporation, what Toni Morrison (1992) calls "whiteness" is "elevated." Qualities taken from the system of "color" are reshaped within whiteness into valued properties of mind and culture. This process leaves a residue that is assigned to the system of color, consisting of undesirable qualities of body and nature. These justify the low position of people of color in the hierarchy of races, and this low rank in turn legitimates their exclusion from resources that are reserved to whiteness. By using Mock Spanish, "Anglos" signal that they possess desirable qualities: a sense of humor, a playful skill with a foreign language, authentic regional roots, an easy-going attitude toward life. The semiotic function by which Mock Spanish assigns these qualities to its Anglo speakers has been called "direct indexicality" by Ochs (1990). "Direct indexicality" is visible to discursive consciousness. When asked about a specific instance of Mock Spanish, speakers will often volunteer that it is humorous, or shows that they lived among Spanish speakers and picked up some of the language, or is intended to convey warmth and hospitality appropriate to the Southwestern region. They also easily accept such interpretations when I volunteer them.

The racist and racializing residue of Mock Spanish is assigned to members of historically Spanish-speaking populations by indirect indexicality (Ochs 1990). Through this process, such people are endowed with gross sexual appetites, political corruption, laziness, disorders of language, and mental incapacity. This semiosis is part of a larger system by which a "fetishized commodity identity" (Vélez-Ibáñez 1992) of these populations is produced and reproduced, an identity which restricts Mexican-Americans and Puerto Ricans largely to the lowest sectors of the regional and national economies. This indexicality is "indirect" because it is not acknowledged, and in fact is actively denied as a possible function of their usage, by speakers of Mock Spanish, who often claim that Mock Spanish shows that they appreciate Spanish language and culture.

The purpose of this paper is to argue for this semiotic analysis of "dual indexicality." The argument, in summary, is that speakers and hearers can only interpret utterances in Mock Spanish insofar as they have access to the negative residue of meaning. Those who hear Mock Spanish jokes, for instance, cannot possibly "get" them—that is, the jokes will not be funny—unless the hearer has instant, unreflecting access to a cultural model of "Spanish speakers" that includes the negative residue. Furthermore, I suggest that Mock Spanish usages actively produce this residue. They carry with them, of course, a debris of racist history that is known to most speakers: they "presuppose," to use Silverstein's (1979) expression, a racist and racialized image. But insofar as speakers laugh at Mock Spanish jokes, or, indeed, interpret Mock Spanish expressions in any of the several appropriate ways, such imagery is also entailed, locally re-produced in the interaction, and thus made available in turn as a presupposition of ensuing interactions.

I suggest that Mock Spanish is a new (at least to the theory of racist discourse) type of what van Dijk (1993) has called "elite racist discourse." While it is often represented as a part of working-class white vernacular, I think that this is incorrect. A few elements of Mock Spanish are unquestionably used by working-class people, especially in the Southwest. But the most productive usage of the system is, I have found, among middle- and upper-income, college-educated whites. Mock Spanish is not heard, nor are printed tokens of it usually encountered, at truck stops, country-music bars, or in the "Employees Only" section of gas stations. Instead, the domain of Mock Spanish is the graduate seminar, the board room, the country-club reception. It is found issuing from the mouths of working-class whites only in the mass media, and is placed there by writers who come from elite backgrounds. I am, myself, a "native speaker" of Mock Spanish. I grew up in West Los Angeles, in a neighborhood where the notoriously wealthy districts of Westwood, Brentwood, and Belair come together. On school playgrounds populated by the children of film directors, real estate magnates, and university professors I learned to say "Adiós" and "el cheapo" and "Hasty banana." The explosion of Mock Spanish that can be heard today in mass media is produced by the highly-paid Ivy-Leaguers who write "The Simpsons," "Roseanne," "Northern Exposure," and *Terminator Two: Judgment Day,* and by the more modest literati who compose greeting-card texts and coffee-cup slogans. This suggests an extremely important property of the large structure of racism—that it is "distributed" within the social system of whiteness. Racist practice in its crudest forms—the obscene insult, the lynching—is assigned within this larger structure to the trailing edge of the upwardly-mobile social continuum of "whiteness." People who overtly manifest such practices are often defined by opinion makers as a minority of "white trash" or "thugs" (even when many surface signs suggest that they are members of the social and economic mainstream). Those who aspire to advancement within whiteness practice instead what is often called "New Racism," the various forms of exclusion and pejoration that are deniable, or justifiable as "fair" or "realistic." The covert practices of Mock Spanish can even be contributed to the system of whiteness by people who are not, personally, racist in any of the usual senses. However, by using Mock Spanish they play their part in a larger racist system, and contribute to its pernicious and lethal effects.

I first review the history of Mock Spanish. I then illustrate contemporary Mock Spanish usage, emphasizing that it constitutes a linguistic system of substantial regularity. In the course of exemplifying this system, I argue for the semiotic interpretation of Mock Spanish as manifesting "dual indexicality" by which desirable qualities are assigned to Anglos, and undesirable qualities are assigned to members of historically Spanish-speaking populations. A number of the examples [in the web version of this article] are illustrated with photographs, and a few are also illustrated with video clips, as indicated in the text. I have discussed several of these examples in previous published work (Hill 1993a and 1993b). However, it was not possible to include illustrations in those publications. The . . . electronic format [of the web version] permits the reader to see some of the evidence that I draw on, and confirm its organization and "feel." For those readers who may not be able to access the illustrations, I provide descriptions and at least partial texts in the discussion below. I conclude with a brief discussion of additional evidence, beyond the semiotic analysis, that Mock Spanish constitutes a racist discourse.

A Brief History of Mock Spanish
Mock Spanish is quite old in American English. The earliest attestation I have found is from the *Dictionary of American Regional English* (Cassidy 1985:508; henceforth, DARE), where we are told that the jail in the city of Mobile was called, in 1792, the "calaboose." This word is from Spanish *calabozo* 'prison' (especially, a subterranean cell, or an isolation cell within a prison). DARE (p. 13) attests the word "Adiós" (from the Spanish farewell) in the full range of senses in Mock Spanish, from the merely "warm" ("The attentive host, who gently waves, with his hand, a final 'ádios' from a window" [Gregg Commerce 156], to the insulting dismissal ("An overworked, spavined, broken-down set—but but adios, Amigo" [*New York Mirror* 23 Dec 208/1, 1837]. This latter sense is especially clear in DARE's passage from Mark Twain's *Screamers,* set in Missouri: "'You are the loser by this rupture, not me, Pie-plant. Adios.' I then left." The DARE attestations also illustrate the national spread of such usages at a very early date. Willem de Reuse has told me about a very interesting example he found in his ethnohistoric research on the Apaches in the 1860's. De Reuse found a reference to a Mexican who was a famous scout for American troops during the Apache wars, named Merejildo Grijalva. Local English speakers called him "Merry Hilda." DARE (p. 411) attests metalinguistic awareness of what I call Mock Spanish as a pejorating and vulgar register at an early period, in a citation for "buckaroo" from Hart's *Vigilante Girl,* set in Northern California: "I can talk what they call 'buckayro' Spanish. It ain't got but thirteen words in it, and twelve of them are cuss words."

Turning to the twentieth century, while DARE provides ample attestations, evidence for my claim that Mock Spanish is especially productive among elites can be found in an article published in *American Speech* in 1949 by a University of Arizona faculty member and a few of his (obviously Anglo) students (Gray, Jones, Parker, Smyth, and Lynd 1949). They attest a wide variety of Mock Spanish greetings and farewells that illustrate the strategy of absurd hyperanglicization: [ædi'yows] 'adios,' "Buena snowshoes" (from *buenas noches* 'Good night'), "Hasty banana" (from *hasta mañana* 'Until tomorrow'), "Hasty lumbago" (from *hasta luego* 'Until later'). Gray and his students suggest that such usages emerged in border towns among knowledgeable Spanish speakers who were mocking the attempts of eastern tourists to pronounce Spanish. This is a very typical rationalization of Mock Spanish and is almost certainly wrong. The importance of the article is the attestation of the intensively productive use of Mock Spanish by Anglo students on a college campus.[4]

The mystery writer Raymond Chandler, who lovingly documented the dark side of Los Angeles in the 1940's and '50's, is credited by critics with a keen ear for the local vernacular. Chandler does not document Mock Spanish in Los Angeles until his 1953 novel *The Long Goodbye*. Attestations of Spanish in earlier novels are placed in the mouths of characters who are Spanish speakers (or pretending to be Spanish speakers, in one case of an aspiring actress who is trying to sound "exotic"). In *The Long Goodbye*, an insulting dismissive greeting occurs when Philip Marlowe, Chandler's long-suffering detective, goes to visit a "Dr. Vukanich," whom he suspects of writing illegal drug prescriptions. The doctor threatens Marlowe with a beating if he doesn't leave. As Marlowe turns to go, Vukanich's speech is represented thus: "Hasta luego, amigo," he chirped. "Don't forget my ten bucks. Pay the nurse" (Chandler 1981 [1953]:131). In this farewell, of course, every word means its opposite: "Hasta luego" ('Until later') means 'Never come back,' and "amigo" does not mean 'friend.'

Today, I think it would be fair to speak of an "explosion" of Mock Spanish. I hear it constantly, and it is especially common at what I call "sites of mass reproduction": films, television shows, including the Saturday morning cartoons watched religiously by most children, greeting cards, video games, political cartoons, coffee-cup slogans intended for display on the office desk, bumper stickers, refrigerator magnets, and the like. These items are marketed far beyond the Southwest.

Mock Spanish as a System of Strategies for Borrowing

Mock Spanish is produced according to quite regular strategies. Before detailing these, it is important to emphasize that Mock Spanish is used almost entirely by Anglo speakers of English, addressed to other Anglos. All parties to the usage can be (and usually are) monolingual speakers of English. The first photograph, Slide 1, is intended to illustrate a usage that is not part of Mock Spanish. It shows a billboard at the corner of First and Glenn, a neighborhood where many Spanish speakers live, and advertises a radio station, KOHT, *La caliente* ('The hot one'), which features eclectic Latin and Anglo selections of music and heavy codeswitching by announcers. The billboard slogan, "*Más música*, less talk" ('More music, less talk') expresses the station's preferred style, which station managers state is intended to be attractive to second- and third-generation Mexican-Americans.[5]

"Mock Spanish" is only one of at least three registers of "Anglo Spanish," which I have detailed in an earlier paper (Hill 1993a). "Cowboy" Spanish is a register of loan words for plants (mesquite), animals (coyote), land forms (mesa), food (tamale), architecture (patio),

SLIDE 1

SLIDE 2

SLIDE 5

legal institutions (vigilante), and (the source of my name for it), an extensive terminology associated with the technology of managing range cattle from horseback, among which the words "lariat" and "bronco" are among the best known. "Cowboy" Spanish is largely restricted to the U.S. southwest, but has some overlap, in both lexicon and usage patterns, with Mock Spanish. The second register is "Nouvelle" Spanish.[6] This is used in marketing the Southwest as "the land of mañana," a place for a relaxing vacation or a peaceful retirement. It produces luxury hotels named "La Paloma," street names in upscale Anglo neighborhoods like "Calle Sin Envidia," and restaurant placemats that wish the diner "Buenas Dias." The grammatical error (it should be "Buen*os* Días") in the last example is quite typical; both Cowboy Spanish and Nouvelle Spanish share with Mock Spanish a more or less complete disregard for the grammatical niceties of any dialect of Spanish itself. Slide 2 shows an especially banal example of Nouvelle Spanish, a small hair salon in a strip shopping center called "Hair Casa."

Mock Spanish itself is a system of four major strategies for the "incorporation" of Spanish-language materials into English. These strategies yield expressions that belong to a pragmatic zone bounded on one end by the merely jocular, and on the other by the obscene insult. They include (1) "Semantic derogation": the borrowing of neutral or positive Spanish loan words which function in Mock Spanish in a jocular and/or pejorative sense; (2) "Euphemism": the borrowing of negative, including scatological and obscene, Spanish words, as euphemisms for English words, or for use in their own right as jocular and/or pejorative expressions; (3) "Affixing": the borrowing of Spanish morphological elements, especially *el* 'the' and the suffix -*o*, in order to make an English word especially jocular and/or pejorative; and (4) "Hyperanglicization": absurd mispronunciations, that endow commonplace Spanish words or expressions with a jocular and/or pejorative sense and can create vulgar puns.

Strategy I: Mock Spanish Semantic Derogation   In "semantic derogation"[7] a positive or neutral Spanish word is borrowed as a Mock Spanish expression and given a humorous or negative meaning. The first two photographs illustrate Mock Spanish uses of the Spanish greeting *Adiós*. In Spanish *Adiós* is an entirely neutral farewell. While it includes the root *Dios* 'God,' it has about as much to do with "God" for most Spanish speakers as English "goodbye," a contraction of "God be with ye," does for English speakers. But it is at the very least polite, and, like "Goodbye," it is not in the least slangy. Slide 3 and Slide 4 are the front and inside of a greeting card from the "Shoebox" division of Hallmark Cards, which is advertised under the slogan "A Tiny Little Division of Hallmark" (one assumes that Shoebox Cards are intended for buyers who see themselves as especially discerning, a bit outside and perhaps above the mainstream). On the front of the card a small figure coded as "Mexican" by his big sombrero and striped serape says, "Adiós."[8] Turning to the inside of the card we find the message shown on Slide 4. The message is not a standard "Best of luck in your new job/house/etc." That is, "Adiós" here is not signaling a laid-back Southwestern warmth. Instead, it is glossed as follows: "That's Spanish for, sure, go ahead and leave your friends, the only people who really care about you, the ones who would loan you their last thin dime, give you the shirts of their backs, sure, just take off!" The second, even more obvious, illustration of the semantic pejoration of "Adiós" is seen in Slide 5. "Adios, cucaracha," with a picture of a fleeing roach, is a bus-bench advertisement for a Tucson exterminating company. The bench is at the corner of Ina and Oracle Roads in one of the most exclusive Anglo neighborhoods, so it is highly unlikely that the ad is addressed to a Spanish-speaking audience. Note that Spanish *cucaracha* is chosen over English "cockroach," to convey heightened contempt.

The final example of "Adiós" appears in a video clip from *Terminator 2: Judgment Day*, a film that made heavy use of Mock Spanish. In the film (at its release in 1991, the most expensive movie ever made) the child "John Connor" must live, because thirty years into the future he will successfully lead a bedraggled band of human survivors in the final war against machines. The machines have twice sent an evil cyborg, a "Terminator," into the past to kill him. But the humans of the future send a good terminator, played by Arnold Schwarzenegger, into the past to protect the boy. The "Adiós" scene is at the end of the film (and at the end of the clip). The Good Terminator has finally destroyed his evil opponent by throwing him into a vat of molten steel. The Good Terminator, John Connor, and Connor's heroic mother Sarah have stolen the arm of the first Terminator (who tried to prevent Connor's conception by killing Sarah!) from scientists who foolishly preserved it for study. The arm must be destroyed, so that the Terminator technology can never threaten humanity. As young Connor tosses the evil artifact into the vat, he says "Adiós." Then we realize that the Good Terminator, whom the humans have come to love and admire, must also destroy himself—his futuristic metal body is as dangerous as those of his evil opponents. Sarah must lower him into the steel. As he descends, he looks one last time at his human friends and says, "Goodbye." The contrast could not be more clear: "Adiós" for evil, "Goodbye" for good.

These uses of "Adiós" cannot be understood except under the "dual indexicality" analysis. By direct indexicality they project variously humor, a streetwise acquaintance with Spanish, a sense of Southwestern regional identity (especially for the greeting card and the advertising sign), and, for the *Terminator 2* screenwriters, a representation of what they take to be the appropriate speech for a white street kid from Los Angeles.[9] Finally, they are all obviously intended as insults. Neither the humor nor the insult is available as a meaning unless a second, indirect, set of indexicals is present. By indirect indexicality these instances of "Adiós" evoke ironically (in the sense suggested by Sperber and Wilson 1981) a greeting that would be uttered by an untrustworthy and insincere person, the kind of person who might stab you in the back, the kind of person who would use a word to mean its opposite. The person thus conjured up is, clearly, a speaker of Spanish. And of course this stereotype, of the sneaky and untrustworthy "Latin lover" or the sneering "Mexican bandit," is undeniably available to American English speakers. Only this presence makes possible the humorous and/or insulting quality of "Adiós" in these usages.[10]

A second derogated Spanish greeting, "Hasta la vista, baby," also appears in *Terminator 2*, from which origin it became an immensely popular slogan that continues to circulate in American usage, in a variety of variants including "Hasta la bye-bye," "Hasta la pasta," and "Hasta la baby, vista."[11] The clip shows the two occurrences in the film. In the first scene, the Good Terminator is driving John Connor and his mother to a desert hideout. The dialogue is as follows:

> MOTHER: Keep it under sixty-five, we don't want to be pulled over.
> TERMINATOR: Affirmative (in a clipped, machine-like tone)
> JOHN CONNOR: No no no no no no. You gotta listen to the way people talk. You don't say "Affirmative," or some shit like that, you say "No problemo." And if someone comes off to you with an attitude, you say "Eat me." And if you want to shine them on, you say, "Hasta la vista, baby."
> TERMINATOR: Hasta la vista, baby (still in a machine-like voice)
> JOHN CONNOR: Yeah, "Later, dickwad." And if someone gets upset, you say, "Chill out," or, you can do combinations.
> TERMINATOR: Chill out, dickwad (in a machine-like voice)
> JOHN CONNOR: That's great! See, you're gettin' it.
> TERMINATOR: No problemo (in a somewhat more natural voice)

This fascinating scene clearly locates Mock Spanish in the same register with extremely vulgar English expressions. But notice that this register, and its Mock Spanish component, is "the way people talk." If the Terminator is to become human, to be redeemed from his machine nature, he must learn to talk this way too. By learning Mock Spanish, the Terminator becomes more like the witty, resourceful young John Connor, and gains the boy's approval. This is a superb demonstration of the direct indexicality of Mock Spanish: it recruits positive qualities to whiteness. However, the indirect indexicality is also made vivid in this passage. By associating "Hasta la vista" with "Eat me" and "Dickwad," an image of Spanish speakers as given to filth and obscenity, and of their language as expressing such qualities, is both presupposed and entailed.

In the next scene we see the most famous token of "Hasta la vista, baby," when Schwarzenegger utters his newly-acquired line as he destroys the evil terminator with a powerful gun.[12] During the 1992 presidential campaign Schwarzenegger, a Republican stalwart, appeared on many occasions in support of President George Bush, uttering the famous line as a threat against Bush's opponents. Bush himself also used the line occasionally. It was used again, by both candidates, in the senatorial campaign conducted in the state of Texas to replace Lloyd Bentsen, who was appointed by Clinton as Secretary of the Treasury. Thus it was clearly judged by campaign managers and consultants as highly effective, resonating deeply with public sentiment.[13] This suggests that the simultaneous pleasures of feeling oneself streetwise and witty, while accessing an extremely negative image of Spanish and its speakers, are widely available to American politicians and voters.

Three further examples illustrate the strategy of semantic derogation. Slide 6 is a political cartoon from the *Arizona Daily Star*, caricaturing Ross Perot, running for President in 1992 against George Bush and Bill Clinton on a third-party ticket. Perot, who is much given to speaking from charts, holds a list that urges support for him because (among other reasons), there are "Bucks flyin into my 'Perot for El Presidente' treasure trove." Here, the direct indexicality is humorous, and permits the comprehending reader to feel cosmopolitan and streetwise. However, the expression is clearly intended to criticize Perot, to suggest that he is pompous and absurd. In order to interpret the insult, the reader must have access to a highly negative image of the sort of person who might be called "El Presidente." This is, of course, the classic tinhorn Latin American dictator, dripping with undeserved medals and presiding in a corrupt and ineffectual manner over a backwater banana republic. Through indirect indexicality, the Mock Spanish expression reproduces this stereotype.

Slide 7, of a "Calvin and Hobbes" comic strip, shows Calvin and his tiger friend Hobbes in one of their endless silly debates about who will be the highest officer in their tree-house club. Hobbes proclaims himself "El Tigre Numero Uno." This is not, however, mere self-aggrandizement; mainly, the locution satirizes the grandiose titles that Calvin makes up for himself, like "Supreme Dictator for Life." Again, by direct indexicality, "El Tigre Numero Uno" is funny, and is also part of Hobbes' cool and witty persona. But to capture the absurdity and the insult, we must also have access to indirect indexicality, which picks out, again, the stereotype of the tinhorn Latin American dictator.

Slide 8 illustrates a very common Mock Spanish usage, of Spanish *nada* 'nothing.' In Mock Spanish the word has been pejorated from this merely neutral meaning into a more extreme sense, meaning 'absolutely nothing.' One formulaic usage, "Zip, zero, nada" (and minor variants) has become wildly popular; I have seen it in television commercials for free drinks with hamburgers, in newspaper announcements for no-fee checking accounts, and, most recently, in an editorial piece in the *Arizona Daily Star* (August 20, 1995) in which an urban planner chastises the Pima County Board of Supervisors for spending "zero dollars—*nada*, zip" on improving a dangerous street intersection (note the classy scholarly italics, present in the original). The comic strip shown in Slide 8, "For Better or for Worse," is by a Canadian artist, and has Canadian content and ambiance. In the strip a group of teenagers are skiing. Gordon "hits on" a pretty girl on the slopes, saying "Hey—What's happening?" She replies, "With you? Nada!!" The Mock Spanish expression seems to heighten the insult over what might be achieved by English "nothing."[14]

Finally, Slide 9 illustrates a common use of semantic derogation, the use of Mock Spanish to express "cheapness" (this is in striking contrast with the most common uses of French in mass media in the United States). Slide 9 is a newspaper advertisement for a sale at Contents, an exclusive furniture store in Tucson. The deep price cuts are announced under the headline "Contemporary and Southwestern Dining, For Pesos." Here, the direct indexicality is not only "light" and jocular; it is almost certainly also invoking regional ambiance. The store flatters its clientele by suggesting that they are "of the Southwest," able

SLIDE 9   SLIDE 10   SLIDE 11

to interpret these Spanish expressions. However, in order to understand how these customers could interpret "For Pesos" (which is surely not intended literally), we must assume that the indirect indexicality presupposed and/or entailed here is that the peso is a currency of very low value. "For Deutschmarks" or "For Yen" would hardly serve the same purpose! This advertisement is dense with Mock Spanish, driving home the message about bargains with, "Si our menu of fine southwestern and contemporary dining tables and chairs at prices that are muy bueno, now during our Winter Sale . . . Plus, caramba, there's Masterplan, our interior design service that helps you avoid costly decorating errors . . . Hurry in today before we say adios to these sale savings, amigo."

The strategy of semantic derogation is highly productive, and includes such well-known expressions as "macho," "the big enchilada," and "No way, José" in addition to the examples above. For every one of these usages, in order to understand how the expression can be properly interpreted, we must assume the division between a set of direct indexes (such as "humorous," "streetwise," "light-hearted," and "regional identity") and a set of indirect indexes which presuppose or entail a highly negative image of the Spanish language, its speakers, and the culture and institutions associated with them.

Strategy II: Mock Spanish Euphemism   The second strategy borrows Spanish words that have highly negative connotations even in the original language, including scatological and obscene expressions. The Mock Spanish form serves as a euphemism for the corresponding rude English word, or creates a new, especially negative semantic space. The first slide illustrating this strategy, Slide 10, is of a coffee cup. Coffee cups bearing silly slogans are popular in many contexts in the United States. They are often the only means of self-expression available to those who toil in offices where the decor of the work space is closely regulated, right down to the color of the blotter, how many pictures can be kept on the desk, and the color and content of posters or prints on the walls. The coffee cup shown was purchased, attractively packaged in its own gift box, in a card and gift shop only a few doors from the University of Arizona campus (the source of many of the items discussed here; the store is, of course, targeting its merchandise at the campus community, thus supporting my claim that Mock Spanish is part of elite usage). The cup bears the slogan, "Caca de Toro," obviously a euphemism for the English expression, "Bullshit." There exist, of course, coffee cups that say "Bullshit," but it seems clear that the "Caca de toro" coffee cup would be more widely acceptable, seen as less vulgar and insulting, than a cup with the English expression. Again, the direct indexicality of this cup is that its owner is a person with a sense of humor, the independence of mind to express a negative attitude, and enough sophistication to understand the Spanish expression (although this expression is not formulaic in Spanish; it is a translation from English). The indirect indexicality required for understanding why the slogan is in Spanish, however, must be that this language is particularly suited to scatology, and that its speakers are perhaps especially given to its use, failing to make the fine distinctions between the polite and the vulgar that might be made by an English speaker.[15] The second illustration of the strategy of borrowing negative Spanish words is seen in Slide 11, of a gift coffee cup bearing the expression "Peon." Unlike

"Caca de Toro," which does not exist as an idiom in Spanish, *peón* is well-established in that language in a negative meaning, originating as the insult *pedón* 'one with large feet,' and referring today to people in low occupations, including foot soldiers and unskilled day laborers. In Latin America it came to designate a person held in debt servitude in a low occupation. The same word is found also in Italian and French (suggesting that the "big-foot" insult was part of the Latin Vulgate), and the English borrowing of the word in the form *peonage* is almost certainly from the last language. The *Oxford English Dictionary* attests *peon* from 1634 (by Samuel Purchas). The *OED* citations all attest a fairly straightforward referential usage of the word in the meaning 'an unskilled laborer,' and include no example of the ironic and insulting sense of the word that is clearly intended on this coffee cup. It is highly unlikely that the anticipated owner of the cup would be 'an unskilled laborer.' Instead, the owner could even be a manager, but would be expressing an ironic complaint about being exploited and maltreated. Indeed, precisely such a sense is clearly attested in my morning paper; in a letter to the *Arizona Daily Star* August 31, 1995, a reader complains about a previous correspondent who argued that people who make low wages (a serious problem in minimum-wage Tucson) do so because they are "lazy and don't care about bettering themselves." The respondent points out that she received a B.A. with honors, but has received no job offers after filing more than 100 applications. She concludes, "Wake up . . . , if you weren't born into the conservative Noble Class before the cutoff date, you are a peon."

While the letter to the editor probably expresses more bitterness than humor, the coffee cup is almost certainly intended to be funny, directly indexing the ability of the owner to laugh at him or herself. Furthermore, the cup expresses a certain courage, since it says something negative about the bosses. Again, however, the indirect indexicality required for full understanding of why a word of known Spanish origin [16] is used for this humorous self-deprecation and complaint must be that the best choice for a prototype for an exploited low status laborer would be one in a Spanish-speaking context.

Slide 12 illustrates a case of the second strategy that is not at all humorous. This slide is the cover of the *Tucson Weekly*, a weekly free newspaper (paid for by advertising) known for its outspoken, even radical, point of view. The cover shows a young Mexican-American man along with the title of the feature article: *Gang-Bangers: La Muerte y la Sangre en el Barrio Centro*, 'Death and Blood in the *Barrio Centro*.' What is curious here is the unusual choice of Spanish for the language of the subtitle; I cannot remember another case where the *Tucson Weekly* used such a long expression in Spanish. Unfortunately, the Spanish title (and the phenotype of the young man in the photograph) suggest a stereotyped association between gang membership and Chicano ethnicity that is not borne out by the facts; many young people in gangs in Tucson are Anglos (and there are also a few African-American gangs). I believe that the Spanish title intends to convey the special direness of the gang threat: "La Muerte y la Sangre" has a sort of Hemingwayesque ring, suggesting that the author of the essay will plumb the most profound depths of the human condition. However, at the same time, the Spanish title has a softening effect—just as "Caca de Toro" is less offensive than "bullshit," "La Muerte y la Sangre" is somehow more distant, less immediate for the English-speaking reader than "Blood and Death." "La Muerte y la Sangre," in short, is something that happens to "Mexican" kids. Here, the direct indexicality thus is probably the sophistication, the ethnographic depth, enjoyed by the author and, in turn, by the reader of the essay. The indirect indexicality is that "muerte" and "sangre" are at the same time more horrible, and yet less serious, than "death" and "blood"—they are, in short, a peculiarly "Spanish" condition capturing some quality of existence in the lower depths that is not available to Anglos in their own language.

The final example of the strategy of euphemism is illustrated by a video clip from the 1992 film *Encino Man*. This film was obviously aimed at young people, and carried, astonishingly, a "PG" rating. The hip (white) teenage subculture of Southern California is apparently viewed by young people across the country as highly attractive, and the film features the actor Pauly Shore, a former MTV announcer, who exemplifies it. Shore is famous for using the variety of English that is closely associated with this subculture, a variety that makes heavy use of Mock Spanish.[17] Indeed, there are far more instances of Mock Spanish in the film than I have space to include. The example that I have chosen is an elaborate and extraordinarily vulgar and obscene joke at the expense of a Chicana character, that is acceptable in a film aimed at children because it is uttered in Spanish. It is an especially clear and dramatic attestation of the Mock Spanish strategy of euphemism.

The plot of *Encino Man* is that two teenage boys who live in Encino (a wealthy suburb of Los Angeles) dig a swimming pool in their backyard and find a Cro-Magnon man encased in a block of ice. They thaw him out, name him "Linc" (as in "Missing"), and take him to high school. The clip opens as "Stoney," Pauly Shore's character, escorts "Linc" to his Spanish class. "Spanish," explains Stoney, "is guacamole, chips, and salsa." Stoney then raises his leg and makes a farting noise. The stereotyped and racist vision of Spanish-speaking culture thus conveyed needs no further comment. Stoney continues in "Spanish": "The dia es mi hermanos, the day is beautiful . . ." (the stereotype reproduced here is that Spanish is a language studied by the dimmest scholars). The two proceed to Spanish class (past a pair of [white!] hip-hoppers), where a supposedly Latina teacher begins an absurd lesson. Grossly mispronouncing the language, the teacher tells the class, "Vale, repítame en esp[æ]ñol: The cheese is old and moldy." The class utters a variety of versions of "El queso está viejo y podrido" (we can hear the last word being pronounced as both "video" and "radio"). The lesson continues with the teacher modeling, "Where is the bathroom, [donde ɛsdá[18] el sanItɛ:Riyow]." The students dutifully repeat this sentence. As the lesson continues, one of the film's absurd "babes" begins flirting with Linc and Stoney. The teacher overhears the clandestine conversation and flicks Stoney hard on his language-class earphones. He objects, "Hey, señorita [ˈseyˈnyoRˀiyˈtə], you hurt my lobes!," with a loud glottal stop before [iyt] that is simultaneously a stereotyped expression of his California white-boy "stoner" character and an absurd and insulting hyperanglicization of *señorita*.

The clip continues with a scene from much later in the film. Stoney and his friend have taken Linc to a bar frequented by cholos, stereotyped as absurd in dress and manner. As the scene opens, the lead cholo threatens Stoney and Dave, warning them not to bother his "muchacha," or he will make sure that they are "no longer recognizable as a man." Linc does not hear the threat, because he is already approaching the cholo's girlfriend, shown as a ridiculous Latin sexpot, writhing hotly in time to the salsa beat of the dance music. Linc grabs the girl and carries her off-screen in classic cave-man style. The cholo finds them dancing together and pulls a knife on Linc, saying, (with subtitles), *Te dije, si yo veo a alguién con mi mujer, lo mato* ("I told you, if I see anybody with my woman, I kill him"). Linc extricates himself from the situation by using the two lines from the morning's Spanish class: "El queso está viejo y podrido. ¿Dónde está el sanitario?" ("The cheese is old and moldy. Where is the bathroom?"). The astounded cholo gapes at him and then begins to laugh. "You're right, *ese*," he chuckles. "She's not worth it!" The girl slaps the cholo, who collapses, weeping, into the arms of his supporters. Just as when, in *Terminator 2: Judgment Day*, the Good Terminator becomes fully human when he learns Mock Spanish, Linc the cave-man is at his most clever and resourceful when he uses the language.

While the direct indexicality of Linc's vulgar joke is positive, enhancing his image, the indirect indexicality of the Spanish in *Encino Man* is almost entirely negative. Indeed, here the indirect indexicality is really not indirect, but fully expressed in the visual images that accompany the talk. The film is trivial and deeply sexist. But what is especially striking about the film is its casual racism: Here, the indirect indexicality projected by the obscene Spanish joke (and by the absurd Spanish class) is amply reinforced by the grossly racist depictions of the cholo and his girlfriend. If similar depictions of African-American characters were to appear in a release from a major studio, there would almost certainly be public outcry. However, as far as I know, *Encino Man* passed quite unnoticed. The implications of this fact for the socialization of white youth are quite horrifying.

There are, of course, innumerable examples of this second strategy. The example of "calaboose" for "jail" discussed above is a case that functions semantically much like "peon." "Cojones" is widely used as a euphemism for the vulgar English "balls." Like semantic pejoration, Mock Spanish euphemism is highly productive, and every case of it I have ever encountered requires the dual-indexicality analysis: Speakers express their sense of humor and cosmopolitanism by direct indexicality, while pejorating and denigrating Spanish language and culture by indirect indexicality, the latter being absolutely required for successful interpretation and appreciation of the humor.

Strategy III: Affixation of Spanish Grammatical Elements   In the third strategy, two elements of Spanish grammar, the definite article *el* and the masculine-gender suffix *-o,* are used with English words to give them a new semantic flavor, ranging from jocularity to insult, or to enhance an already somewhat negative connotation of the English word. Slide 13 is a picture of the box for a piece of software for personal computers, called "El Fish." Using "El Fish," one can create a picture of an aquarium with water plants, decorative miniature figurines and buildings, and swimming fish. The software offers a diverse menu for each component of the aquarium, permitting many different combinations. The on-screen effect is surprisingly attractive, and "El Fish" was very popular in the early 1990's. The interest here, of course, is that the software is called "El Fish" as a joke, because the fish are not "real" fish, but simulated fake fish. Again, we see the split indexicality, between the direct projection of mildly self-deprecating humor, and the indirect presupposition that something labeled in Spanish is cheap and of lower quality.

The very common Mock Spanish expression "No problemo" (that we already encountered in the first scene from the video clip from *Terminator 2: Judgment Day*) is an excellent example of this strategy. The source here is not Spanish; instead, this is the result of *-o* suffixing. The Spanish word meaning "problem" is *problema,* not *problemo.*[19] Furthermore, there is no Spanish formula *No X;* one must say *No hay X.* So the source of this expression must be the colloquial English expression, "No problem." By adding *-o,* this expression is made "lighter," more humorous. "No problemo" is ubiquitous. Slide 14 is an advertisement for a candy store in Tucson, but Slide 15 illustrates a cartoon from *The New Yorker* magazine, entitled "God's Subcontractors." In the last panel, God's "Animal man" says, "You want animals? No problemo."

While "No problemo" is perhaps the most frequent example of *-o* suffixing in Mock Spanish, the technique is extraordinarily productive, far beyond standard examples such as "el cheap-o" for an especially low-quality product. Once, browsing in my university bookstore, I overheard the following remark made by an employee to her colleagues: "I'm going to lunch now. Bye, guys, sell mucho bookos." (Here, the use of Mock Spanish "mucho," which is extremely common and probably exemplifies the first strategy, but which is also interpretable as a case of *-o* affixing to an English word.) A colleague, criticizing a sister department for its approach to undergraduate education, proclaimed, "Over there, it's all T.A.'s. Period-o [piRi'owdow]. No professors." A particularly interesting example comes

SLIDE 14

from the student-run newspaper at the University of California at San Diego; it is a "Personal ad" that reads as follows: "Don Thomas—Watcho your backo! You just mighto wake uppo con knee capo obliterato. Arriba!" [20]

The frame "Numero X-o" is highly productive. "Numero uno" is of course common, lending a jocular tone to enumeration, or rendering more colloquial a proclamation that some entity is "Number one" ("the best of its kind"). A virtuoso user of this type of enumeration is Joe Bob Briggs, for several years a columnist for the Dallas *Times-Herald,* where he created a hilarious column in which he reviewed drive-in movie monster and horror films, using the persona of a sex- and violence-crazed redneck. The columns (which have been collected in a book (Briggs 1987) are dense with Mock Spanish, including enumeration (usually of the erotic and violent qualities of the films) up to "Numero ten-o," "Numero eleven-o," and the like. The well-known political columnist Molly Ivins was Briggs's colleague on the *Times-Herald,* and her own use of this enumeration frame in her columns in the service of the creation of a colloquial Texas English is probably borrowed from him. [21] In summary, examples of this third strategy again provide evidence for the split indexicality analysis: in order to "get" the humor of these usages, an indirect indexicality of denigration of Spanish and its speakers is required.

Strategy IV: Hyperanglicization and Bold Mispronunciation   For those readers of this paper who have never heard Mock Spanish, it is important to know that it is almost always pronounced in entirely English-language phonology; Mock Spanish cannot be understood as "code-switching" in the usual sense. However, Mock Spanish forms are often more than merely Anglicized. Instead, they undergo what I call (Hill 1993a) "hyperanglicization," yielding pronunciations that are widely known to be ludicrous departures from their Spanish originals. These absurd mispronunciations provide a rich source of vulgar puns, some of them best rendered in writing, as in the following examples.

Slides 16 and 17 show a Christmas card (it is printed on environmentally-sensitive recycled paper, as are many of my Mock Spanish greeting cards). Slide 16 shows the front of the card, with the legend "Pablo, the Christmas Chihuahua, has a holiday wish for you" over a drawing of a ludicrously ugly little dog wearing a huge sombrero and scratching frantically at the many fleas visibly jumping around on his hairless body. The greeting inside the card (Slide 17) is "Fleas Navidad," a pun on the Spanish Christmas salutation, *Feliz Navidad.* The second pair of slides is of a thank-you card. Slide 18 shows the front of the card, with a tiny mouse crouching in a sea of grass, and the word "Muchas" ('Many'). Opening the card (Slide 19), we find more grass and the word "Grass-ias," a hyperanglicized version of Spanish *gracias* 'Thanks' that yields the pun. [22] Slides 20 and 21 show a birthday card; the front shows a cow, clad in sombrero and serape. The greeting inside is "Happy Birthday to a guy who's 'Moo-cho terrifico.'" This card, of course, illustrates the third and fourth strategies together. [23]

Slide 22 is from a Calvin and Hobbes comic strip. Hobbes is teasing Calvin by pretending that the detested little neighbor girl, Susie, has sent Calvin a Valentine's Day card. As Calvin reads the mushily romantic greeting, Hobbes rubs in the insult by gloating, "Muchas Smooches for el con-kiss-tador!" Slide 23 reproduces a menu from a Mexican restaurant in Tucson. This slide requires brief contextualization. Tucson enjoys many very good and quite serious Mexican restaurants, some of them internationally famous for authentic and creative development of this cuisine. The best are on the south-central side of town, in neighborhoods with many Spanish-speaking residents. "Baja Bennie's," the source for this menu, is on the very far north-east side in an area that is notoriously almost exclusively Anglo. It is a favorite place for young Anglo professionals. The Baja Bennie's menu parodies the menus in legitimate Mexican-food venues with silly Mock Spanish section headings like "El Figuro Trimmo." This section is explained as "Bennie's answer to the 'Border Patrol,' sort of our Mex-er-size area . . . ," a note that would be interpreted as the grossest sort of insult by almost any Chicano. The menu parodies the "pronunciation guides" that are sometimes found on Mexican restaurant menus; the section entitled

SLIDE 23

"Especiales de Casa" (instead of *Especialidades de la casa*) is followed by the parenthetical "(spesh-al tees)."

My final example for the strategy of hyperanglicization is a video of a very complex and ambivalent skit from the television program "Saturday Night Live."[24] The skit features the well-known Latino actor Jimmy Smits, a role model for youth who is frequently featured in literacy and anti-drug campaigns. The skit opens in a conference room where a television news program is finishing up; the reporter closes her story with the words, "This is Robin Fletcher, reporting live from Managua, Nicaragua." "Robin Fletcher" pronounces the place name in a reasonable approximation of educated second-language Spanish. This line, however, opens the way for an increasingly absurd performance, in which members of the cast pronounce everyday names for places and people that have standard Anglicizations in exaggeratedly phony Spanish accents. For instance, one character uses [horr'ʈega] for "Ortega." Into the middle of this absurdity comes Jimmy Smits, who is introduced as "Antonio Mendoza," an economics correspondent. One male cast member shows off his Spanish expertise, asking the new arrival whether he should pronounce his name [men'dosa] or as Castilian [men'doθa]. Smits replies mildly that [mEn'dowsdh@] (the normal Anglicization) would be fine, or even [mɛn'dowzə]. Mexican food is delivered, yielding another round of absurd pronunciations. "Mendoza" observes that the others present really like Latino food; one character proudly announces that his taste for such food was developed growing up in [loh 'hangeles]. Next, the famous sportscaster Bob Costas appears in a cameo role, introduced as "Bob ['kosʈas]." He is briefly quizzed about his predictions for the coming Sunday's football games, with absurd pronunciations of team and place names ([brrronkos], [ʈampa] Bay, [san frrran'siysko]), until he is called out of the room because he has left the lights on in his car, a [ka'mahrrro]. "Antonio Mendoza" listens to these performances with increasing consternation, finally volunteering, "You guys really seem to be up on your Spanish pronunciation. But if you don't mind my saying, sometimes when you take Spanish words and kind of over-pronounce them, well, it's kind of annoying." Stunned, one offender asks him to explain what he means. "Well," says "Mendoza," "you know that kind of storm that has winds that whirl round and round?" "Of course," answers the butt, "a [torrrr'na:dðo]." "Mendoza" shrugs his shoulders and gives up. Then another actor offers him Mexican food. Mendoza has declined before, but he says, "OK, I guess I'll have an [ɛnčI'laDə]" (in the normal Anglicization). The other actor says, "What?" Mendoza repeats, still mildly and politely: "An [ɛnčI'laDə]. I said, I'll have an [ɛnčI'laDə]." The other actor still refuses to understand him, and "Mendoza" loses it finally, leaping to his feet and shouting, "An [e:nči'la:ða]! [an:'to:nyo men'do:sa] would like an [e:nči'la ða]! It would be very muy bueno because [an:'to:nyo] is very ['ha:ngri:]! It would make him feel really good to have an [e:nči'laða]!" The other actors nod approvingly at one another, observing "Hey, this guy's all right!" The skit ends.

I have played this video clip several times to academic audiences consisting largely of Anglos, and it never fails to get huge laughs—indeed, the hilarity from the early examples makes many of the later ones inaudible. I think the skit permits the release in laughter of some of the discomfort such people feel about Spanish. Hyperanglicization in Mock Spanish can be partly explained as expressing this discomfort, and as constructing a "distance" between the pronouncer and the language that is endowed with low status by repeated parody. The ambivalence is especially acute for academics, who may not want to seem ignorant about Spanish pronunciation. The skit also seems to imply that Anglos who try for a correct pronunciation, like the "Robin Fletcher" television reporter who opens the skit, are out of line and should stick to good all-American Anglicized versions of place names and personal names. Under this interpretation, Jimmy Smits is in fact playing into the hands of anti-Spanish sentiment. However, I am told by Spanish-speaking Americans that the skit has, for them, quite different readings. The "Antonio Mendoza" character expresses for them their own negative feelings about English accents in Spanish, which they find grating. Further, they understand the character as sharing their resentment at the fact that Anglos with even moderate skills in Spanish are admired as highly educated, and are clearly proud of their linguistic sophistication, while their own greatly superior knowledge of the language is suspected of being "unamerican," or taken as a mark of inferiority. Finally, the Smits character expresses exasperation that he cannot be an ordinary "economics consultant," but has to play out an image of being "Chicano" that will satisfy Anglos. On any reading, the skit captures the extreme ambivalence and complexity of ideologies about Spanish in the United States.

Hyperanglicized examples of Mock Spanish are nearly always interpretable only under the analysis of split indexicality developed above. However, they add an additional dimension to the indirect indexicality: hyperanglicized pronunciation expresses iconically the extreme social distance of the speaker, and of Mock Spanish itself, from actual Spanish and any possible negative contamination that a speaker might acquire by being erroneously heard as a real speaker of Spanish.[25]

Further Evidence for Racism in Mock Spanish

Thus far, I have argued that Mock Spanish is ineluctably racist because it can only be understood by speakers insofar as they have access to its indirect indexical force, of relentless denigration of the Spanish language, culture, and people. However, there is additional evidence that Mock Spanish is a racist discourse.

Occasionally Mock Spanish usage reveals its fundamental character by being embedded in grossly racist texts. I owe one example to Jodi Goldman, who found an article from *The Koala*, the University of California at San Diego student satirical newspaper, from April 6, 1994. This satirical piece requires contextualization: college students from institutions along the border often choose to spend "Spring Break" at beach resorts in Mexico, a dislocation which many take as an excuse to go on an alcohol-fueled orgy of misbehavior that is a source of exasperation to Mexicans and enormous concern to college officials and parents in the United States (serious injuries and even deaths are unfortunately not rare). The article in *The Koala* is a fantasy about being arrested on a beer-sodden Spring Break at Rosarita Beach in Baja California, and is entitled "¿Que pasa en tus pantalones?" The author provides a parodic "pronunciation guide" to her name: "By Pamela Benjamin (Pronounced: Pahm-eh-lah Ben-haam-een)." The article features many elaborate instances of Mock Spanish, but I will restrict myself to one revealing paragraph, which the author introduces by noting that "I have no knowledge of Spanish." She continues:

> *My brother taught me a few phrases: "Cuanto cuesta es tu Madre?" (How much does your mother cost?), "Que pasa en tus pantalones?" (What's happening in your pants?), and the answer for that question, "Una fiesta en mi pantalones, y tu invito." (There's a party in my pants, and you're invited.) These phrases were of no help to me when captured by*

Mr. Hideous, Huge-sweat-rings-on-his-uniform, Body-oder[sic]-of-a-rotting-mule, Must-eat-at-least-10-tortas-a-day, Mexican Federale guy. I thought I was going to die, not only from his smell, but from the killer cockroaches the size of hamsters in the back seat. I thought to myself, "No problem, Pam. You can deal with this. Stay calm, don't scream, and say something in Spanish. He'll notice your amazing brilliance and let you go." Unfortunately, the first thing that popped out was, "Cuanto Cuesta es tu Madre?" My doom was sealed.

Here, one hardly needs the "dual indexicality" analysis: Mexico is clearly depicted as a corrupt and filthy country, where the only Spanish one needs are the few phrases necessary to buy the services of a prostitute.

Mock Spanish in print is very frequently associated with patently racist imagery. Several slides illustrate the association of Mock Spanish with racist imagery. First are two greeting cards that are "bean jokes." "Beaner" is a racist epithet for Mexican American. The clip from *Encino Man* shows the "Stoney" character pretending to fart as he describes Mexican food. "Bean jokes" in Mock Spanish clearly associate Spanish and its speakers with the lowest and most vulgar forms of humor. Slides 24 and 25 show the front and inside of a greeting card (on recycled paper). On the front the words "¿Como frijoles?" are spelled out in small brown beans. The inside of the card translates this with the pun, "How have you bean?"[26] Slide 26 shows a "Mexican," dressed in huge sombrero, serape, and white pajama-like suit, jumping over a bean, over the caption "Mexican Jumping Bean." Above this picture is the word "Amigo." Opening the card, we find the greeting, "Señor friend a letter, or I'll never get over it." The image of a stereotyped "Mexican" shown on this greeting card (it also appears on the "Adios" card in Slide 3) is repeated on slides 27 and 28. The front of this Christmas card (from the same series as the one featuring "Pablo, the Christmas Chihuahua") shows barefoot "Mexicans," wearing huge sombreros and shaking maracas, singing "Deck the halls with hot frijoles, 'tis the season to eat tamales." Inside the card (Slide 29) reads, "Fa la la la la, la bamba." Slide 30 shows a card by the famous cartoonist Gary Larson. An enormous Tyrannosaurus, dressed in huge sombrero and serape, looms across a river from a wary herd of vegetarian dinosaurs. The caption reads, "However, there was no question that on the south side of the river, the land was ruled by the awesome Tyrannosaurus mex." The card not only reproduces a racist image; it also uses the vulgar epithet "Mex," which can hardly be uttered in polite discourse today (here, of course, the excuse is to make the pun on "rex"). The card is probably intended to poke fun at worries about immigration from Mexico, but it does so by using imagery and language that reproduce the racialization of Mexicans.

Many Mexican-Americans find caricatures of Mexicans hidden under huge sombreros to be grossly offensive. They have precisely the force for them that the picture of a grinning black boy with a slice of watermelon, or a fat-cheeked mammy with her head done up in a kerchief, have for African Americans. Following many years of effort by Latino citizens' groups, this image has been largely eliminated from mainstream advertising and mass media (an important example was the agreement by the Frito-Lay Corporation to give up its trademark caricature of the "Frito Bandido"). However, it survives vigorously in a variety of minor media such as on these greeting cards.[27]

Teun van Dijk, in *Elite Discourse and Racism,* argues that in a theory of racist discourse it is essential to take into account what he calls "minority competence," the assessment of a situation, as racist or non-racist, by "those who *experience* racism as such, that is, the competent or 'conscious' members of minority groups" (van Dijk 1993:18). This is a fundamental departure from the tradition that regards the views of the targets of racism as unreliable, because biased. Instead, it suggests that we view competent members of minority communities as especially likely to be able to make nuanced discriminations between racist and non-racist or anti-racist practice, because it is precisely they who have the most at stake in making such distinctions. Van Dijk recognizes that there may be wide variation among minority-group members in general. I have never addressed an audience on this topic without having an Anglo member of the audience tell me that my analysis is incorrect, because a Mexican-American or Puerto Rican friend of theirs once sent them a card, or told them a joke, with Mock Spanish content. I have no doubt that they are telling the truth about their experiences. Certainly some Mexican-Americans find the tokens of Mock Spanish that I have shown them (including many of the items described above) to be entertaining. However, I find that those Mexican-Americans who laugh at Mock Spanish are generally very young (many of them have been college freshmen or sophomores) or relatively naive and uneducated. Older people are almost unanimous in immediately reacting negatively to these tokens. Many of them recognize the Mock Spanish genre immediately, and volunteer stories about times that Anglos have offended them by using Mock Spanish to them, such as calling them "Amigo" or asking them "Comprende?" One Mexican-American colleague, the business manager in a neighboring unit, has an absolutely accurate eye for good examples and has found some of my best attestations. She finds Mock Spanish advertising to be offensive and disrespectful. Raúl Fernández, a Professor of Chicano Studies at the University of California-Irvine, shared with me a letter to the editor that he wrote to the *Los Angeles Times,* objecting to the use of the word "cojones" in a film review (I do not know if the letter was printed). Fernando Peñalosa pointed out many years ago, in his book *Chicano Sociolinguistics* (1980), that the egregiously ungrammatical and misspelled public uses of Spanish that he identified in Southern California, including place names and public notices, were a manifestation of racism.[28] In summary, thoughtful people among the Latino and Chicano population in the Southwest usually define Mock Spanish as a racist practice.[29]

Conclusion: Mock Spanish Is a New Kind of Elite Racist Discourse
I have shown that Mock Spanish usages cannot be interpreted unless interlocutors reproduce, through indirect indexicality, very negative images of Spanish and its speakers. It functions, therefore, as a racist discourse in itself. I have also shown that uses of Mock Spanish often co-occur with grossly racist imagery, as in the film *Encino Man,* and in greeting cards showing stereotyped "Mexicans." Furthermore, I have shown that many Mexican-Americans of my acquaintance concur that it is racist, and I have argued, following van Dijk (1993), that their views must be taken very seriously. However, I have found in discussing this work that many Anglos find my conclusions implausible. How, they argue, can Mock Spanish be racist? They use it, and they are not racist. Molly Ivins uses it; surely she is not racist. How could anyone call "Calvin and Hobbes" a racist comic strip, or *Terminator 2: Judgment Day* a racist film? I would argue, along with many contemporary theorists of racism such as van Dijk (1993), Essed (1991), and Goldberg (1993), that to find that an action or utterance is "racist," one does not have to demonstrate that the racism is consciously intended. Racism is judged, instead, by its effects: of successful discrimination and exclusion of members of the racialized group from goods and resources enjoyed by members of the racializing group. It is easy to demonstrate that such discrimination and exclusion not only have existed in the past against Mexican Americans and other members of historically Spanish-speaking populations in the United States, but continue today. Furthermore, the semiotic analysis that I have proposed above demonstrates that Mock Spanish is discriminatory and denigrating in its indexical meaning, that it cannot be understood without knowing about the stereotypes that such indexes presuppose and entail, even if speakers believe that what they are doing is inoffensive joking. Mock Spanish is effective precisely because of its relative deniability, because people are not aware of "being racist," even in a mild way, let alone in a vulgar way. Through its use, the "upwardly mobile system of whiteness" is created covertly, through the indirect indexicality of hundreds of taken-for-granted commonplace utterances that function to "racialize" their targets, constructing them as members of a human group represented as essentially inferior. Elinor Ochs (1990) argued that it is through these covert indexes that the deepest structures of the self, those that are least accessible to inquiry and modification, are laid down. Indeed, the notion that covert semiosis is at least as, if not more, powerful than overt meaning in the construction

of the world through linguistic practice goes back in linguistics and anthropology through the work of Silverstein (1979) to that of Whorf and even before.

A second argument that is often used against my analysis is that there are in American English many expressions that mock other languages besides Spanish. This is, of course, correct. One can hear Americans say "beaucoup trouble" and "Mercy Buckets," just as one can hear them say "mucho trouble" and "Much Grass." "Spinmeister" mocks German, and "refusenik" plays with Russian. It seems to me obvious, however, that these other "mock" usages are today scattered and relatively unproductive, in stark comparison with Mock Spanish. The only register of borrowing that seems to me to be even remotely comparable is that of jocular Yiddish. Jocular Yiddish is, however, used by people with a claim on a Yiddish-speaking heritage, quite unlike Mock Spanish, which is used almost exclusively by English speakers, most of them monolingual.

Finally, I suggest that "Mock Spanish" constitutes a new type of racist discourse. The kinds of examples that van Dijk (1993) treats as illustrations of "elite racist discourse" are nearly all far more overt, addressing directly whether privileges and rights (such as immigration, or access to public housing) should be extended to members of racialized populations. For instance, van Dijk points out that elite racist discourse can be identified when it is accompanied by qualifying expressions. Someone might say: "Of course I don't dislike foreigners, some of them are fine people, but our country has already admitted too many immigrants." Even though such a speaker would deny that the statement "Our country already has too many immigrants" was racist, the qualifying statement shows that the speaker knows that it could be heard in that way, rather than only an absolutely neutral scientific judgment that shows that the speaker is in control of statistical evidence about what percentage of immigrants is optimal for national development. People who use Mock Spanish do not use such qualifying expressions. Nobody would say, "Of course Arnold Schwarzenegger has many Mexican-American friends, but he said 'Hasta la vista, baby' at the rally for Bush." Or, "I have the highest respect for the Mexican people, but no problemo." Or, "Excuse the expression, but, numero two-o. . . ." These facts enlarge our understanding of the continuum of racist discourse. A picket sign that says "Wetbacks go home!" is obvious vulgar racism. Van Dijk has demonstrated that expressions like, "I don't have anything against Mexicans as such. But we can't pay to deliver the baby of every pregnant lady in Mexico who wants her kid to be an American citizen" constitute clear cases of "elite racist discourse." To these two types we need to add a third, at the most covert end of the continuum, reproducing racism almost entirely through indirect indexicality. This type is exemplified by cases like "Hasta la vista, baby." The first is easily identifiable as racist and is almost always avoided by the powerful; indeed, public vulgar racism precisely indexes powerlessness. The second sounds sleazy and weasely to many thoughtful Anglos. But the last seems to most Anglos to be utterly innocent, even delightful and clever. I would argue, however, that this last is the most powerful of the three. Because of its seeming innocence, it can find its way into a film seen by literally hundreds of millions of people, and can become a clever new casual expression, functioning in that useful range of meanings that range between light talk and insult, that is used by everyone from six-year-olds to senatorial candidates. And each time that it is used, it inexorably reproduces a highly negative stereotype of speakers of Spanish.

American racism almost certainly includes other, similar strategic systems that might be identified by careful research. Especially, similar devices that function to pejorate and racialize African Americans and Asian Americans should be sought and analyzed. Furthermore, many questions remain about Mock Spanish itself. For instance, its history needs more careful investigation. We need to develop techniques by which to show when it has been more, and when less, intense and productive, and whether this ebb and flow of productivity coincides with economic cycles or other possibly related phenomena. More information is needed about who uses Mock Spanish. I have concluded, on the basis of limited and informal observation, that it is largely an elite usage, but it may be extending its reach across the social organization of the system of Whiteness. What are its functions in parts of the English-speaking world like Canada and Ireland (a friend has pointed out to me instances in the novels of Roddy Doyle), where Spanish-speaking populations are minuscule and largely irrelevant to the local racist system? Furthermore, Mock Spanish raises a whole range of fascinating questions about the role of humor in discrimination. One of the most compelling arguments of conservative foes of what is called "Political Correctness" is that the "politically correct" have no sense of humor.[30] It strikes me that vulgar racism, for those who practice it, also seems to be fun, full of shared humor. Signs saying "No Mexicans or Dogs served here" were obviously intended to be hilarious. The Good Old Boys at a recent weekend retreat of "law enforcement officers" featured on the national news probably found the "Nigger Check Point" sign (assuming that it was really there, and not faked by their enemies) to be a real thigh-slapper. The drunken laughter of the lynch mob is a stereotype of American history. Unlike the deadly serious, careful register of "elite racist discourse" that van Dijk has identified, systems like Mock Spanish share humor uncomfortably with the cackling of the mob, in the snickering of the corner boys as one of their number sticks out a foot and trips up a black man. How important is humor and joking in the reproduction of racism? (And, of course, of sexism, anti-Semitism, and other systems of discrimination and exclusion). In summary, much remains to be done. I believe that linguistic anthropologists are especially well-qualified, by the power and subtlety of the analytical tools that are available to us today, to make progress in these matters that are so important to the health of our society.

NOTES

1. In some previous papers on this phenomenon (cf. Hill 1993b), and in several lectures, I referred to this system as "Junk Spanish." I found that this term was very frequently misunderstood as a reference to so-called "Border Spanish," the code-switching, somewhat anglicized forms of Spanish that can be heard from some speakers in the U.S. Southwest. I am indebted to James Fernandez for a very convincing explanation of why this misunderstanding was so pervasive, and for the suggestion of "Mock Spanish." Fernandez points out that for English speaker the association between "junk"—ruin and decline—and the Mediterranean areas of Europe (and the colonial offshoots) is hundreds of years old. The use of "junk" plays into this system. "Mock" both avoids this metaphorical system and makes clearer the central function and social location of the register of English that I address here.

2. The term "Anglo" is widely used in the Southwest for "white people." It is an all-encompassing term that includes Italians, Greeks, Irish, etc. Its existence (it is a short, monomorphemic element) is eloquent testimony to the social reality of this group, the members of which often like to argue that they are too diverse internally for such a single label. I will use

this term for this social unit in the remainder of the paper.

3. In Arizona, "Official English" legislation, pushed by the national organization U.S. English, took the form of an amendment to the state constitution that included particularly restrictive language, that in the business of "the state and all its dependencies" (which include the University of Arizona), officers of the state (which includes me), "shall act in English and in no other language." The only exclusions were for the criminal courts, the teaching of foreign languages, and health and safety emergencies. Both the federal district court and the Ninth Circuit Court of Appeals have held this amendment to be in violation of the first and fourteenth amendments of the U.S. Constitution. Woolard (1989) is an excellent treatment of the ideological foundations of a comparable statute passed in California.

4. Mock Spanish continues to be a source of campus humor; I hear it frequently at the University of Arizona, and it is documented in the everyday usage of Anglo students at the University of California at San Diego in a project recently concluded by Kathryn Woolard and her students. I thank Kathryn Woolard for sharing with me these materials.

5. Note, however, that KOHT's billboard does have an intertextual relationship with Mock Spanish, and is almost certainly based on a "More X, less Y" frame that comes from English. An unquestionably Mock Spanish usage of the same structure was passed on to me by my colleague Maria Rodriguez. A flyer advertising a Mexican-food restaurant features the slogan "Mas Dinner, Less Dinero" ("More dinner, less money"). This slogan echoes the Mock Spanish strategy of adding Spanish morphology to an English word to form the "Dinner/Diner-o" pun, and also makes a characteristic association of Spanish with cheapness. The rest of the text of the ad is entirely in English, and the two branches of the restaurant are located in Anglo neighborhoods on the north side of Tucson.

6. This name borrows from "Nouvelle Southwest Cuisine," a kind of food that includes items like lobster fajitas with mango salsa, and chiles rellenos stuffed with pistachio nuts, goat cheese, and sundried tomatoes.

7. I take this expression from the work of Muriel Schulz (1975) on the historical semantic trajectory of words with female referents, such as "queen" (which has acquired the sense of "transvestite," in contrast to "king") and "housewife" (which has the contracted offshoot "hussy," in contrast to "husband," which has no such derogated relative).

8. The correct use of the accent mark on the *o* here is nothing short of astonishing. Written Mock Spanish is usually orthographically absurd.

9. "John Connor" has been "raised up rough" by an aunt and uncle, since his mother is locked in a lunatic asylum because she keeps talking about the first terminator. He is represented at the beginning of the film as running wild in the streets. I have no idea whether working-class white kids in Los Angeles today actually talk like John Connor. I do know, however, that the exposure of the screenwriters of such a film to the talk of kids is far more likely to be at the catered birthday party in Bel Air or in the parking lot of the Montessori School than on the actual mean streets of L.A.

10. There is no doubt that "Adios" is also used, at least in the Southwest, when speakers wish merely to be "warm" rather than funny and insulting. In this case, the stereotype of "Mexicans" (or perhaps the stereotype is of some gruff old Anglo rancher from the 1860's who has helped you fight off the Apaches) is that of generosity and hospitality. This usage does not, of course, cancel out the force of the very common use of "Adios" to convey insult.

11. I owe the "Hasty la baby, vista" example to Jodi Goldman, who found it in *The Koala*, a satirical newspaper published by UCSD students, in the March 8, 1993 edition. The phrase appears in an ad parodying the advertising for "Terminator 2: Judgement Day." I thank Kathryn Woolard for sending me the work of Ms. Goldman and other students.

12. In the film, the miraculous properties of the terminator metal permit the pieces of the evil terminator's shattered body to flow together and reconstitute him; he comes after Schwarzenegger and his charges again! This detail is neglected by politicians who use "Hasta la vista, baby" as an expression for final dismissal.

13. In Texas, the Democratic candidate Robert Krueger used "Hasta la vista, baby" in a television commercial where he dressed in a peculiar black suit apparently intended to allude to "Zorro," a sort of Robin-Hood-like Mexican bandit from 1950's television. This commercial was considered especially absurd, and did nothing to dispel Krueger's reputation as a panty-waist college professor who was hopelessly distant from the Schwarzenegger image.

14. Illustrating the presence of such usages among elites, and attesting again to their geographical spread, I was informed by a colleague who teaches in a university in the northeastern U.S. (in a city with many Spanish speakers) that the graduate admissions committee in her department referred to the stack of rejected applications as the "Nada pile." They've now changed the name. At the other end of the social continuum, "nada" provides one of the few examples of Mock Spanish that I have heard from a person whom I would evaluate as perhaps working class. I was trying to pick up a prescription at the pharmacy in a nearby grocery store that is located in a neighborhood that is distinctly downscale. When the pharmacist's assistant (who might have been 18 or 20) couldn't find my prescription, she returned to her register and told me "Nada."

15. Spanish is, of course, by no means the only European language that is used as a source of "softened" scatological and obscene expressions for English speakers; one thinks immediately of Yiddish *dreck* and French *merde*. But

Mock Spanish is a far more productive source. Another example along the same lines is a Mock Spanish version of the widely-distributed slogan "Shit Happens," seen on bumper stickers and other paraphernalia. Bumper stickers are available that read "Casa Pasa."

16. It would be useful to have clear evidence that most English speakers believe that this word is Spanish (as opposed to, say, Old French). I believe that this is the case. I remember studying Mexico and learning that its "haciendas" had "peons" in the fifth or sixth grade!

17. I am indebted to Jay Sanders for drawing my attention to the use of Mock Spanish by Southern California teens; he contributed to a course in Discourse Analysis tapes of young female friends of his (who were from Thousand Oaks, not Encino), chatting casually on the phone using unusually high frequencies of Mock Spanish. Pauly Shore has made several films since "Encino Man" that probably deserve attention as well.

18. The pronunciation "No problem[ə] also exists; I have the impression that "No problemo" is more common.

19. This personal ad may have beep attempting a parody of a "Sicilian Mafia" usage. But the "Arriba!" definitely suggests that Mock Spanish has swamped "Mock Sicilian." I owe this example to Kathryn Woolard.

20. I owe this suggestion about the relationship between Ivins and Briggs to Don Brenneis.

21. There is another, more vulgar version of this greeting that I have not seen. I owe the description of it to Barbara Babcock, who received a card where the front showed Hawaiian hula dancers, face forward, and the word "Muchas." Opening the card revealed a rear view of the dancers, buttocks clearly visible through their grass skirts, and the word "Grassy-ass."

22. The treatment of the Spanish syllable *mu-* as English "moo," complete with cow, is attested in several examples collected by Woolard's students at the University of California at San Diego. Jodi Goldman found a (presumably "Christian") bookmark featuring a picture of a cow reading a book entitled "God is MOOOY BUENO." Gina Gemello reported a billboard for Clover Dairy (in the San Francisco Bay area), that featured a cow saying "Moooy Bueno."

23. I thank Gerardo López Cruz for providing me with a copy of his video of this skit.

24. I develop this point at greater length in Hill (1993a).

25. Susan Philips found a card that actually shows a "Mexican" sleeping under an enormous sombrero, under the question, "¿Cómo esta frijol?" (Punctuation as in the original). Inside, the Card reads: "[English translation] How ya bean?" (Of course it is printed on 100% recycled paper.)

26. A particularly egregious example occurred on the 1994 Christmas gift wrap chosen by a local store, "Table Talk." Many items in the store were prewrapped in a dark green paper that featured howling coyotes and striped snakes wearing bandanas, and a repeated figure of a "Mexican" asleep under his sombrero, leaning against a saguaro cactus. Diego Navarette reported to me that he actually complained at one Table Talk branch, and received an apology from the manager and a promise that the offending wrap would be withdrawn. However, when I visited the store just before Christmas, the offending wrap was still available for custom wrapping, and the prewrapped gifts were still stacked in the aisles as part of the Christmas decor.

27. Dominique Louisor-White and Dolores Valencia Tanno (1994), of the Communications department at California State University at San Bernardino, found that Mexican-American television newscasters in the Los Angeles area were increasingly likely to choose fully Spanish pronunciations of names when reading the news, starting with the pronunciation of their own names, since they regarded the usual Anglicized pronunciations as disrespectful. (They often encountered opposition to their pronunciation from Anglo station managers.)

28. Members of historical Spanish-speaking populations do not, in my experience, use Mock Spanish much when speaking English. I have heard such a usage only once, when a highly-placed Mexican American man, prominent and powerful in the Tucson community, said "Adios" as an Anglo subordinate left a meeting. Certainly such people code-switch frequently from English to Spanish when talking to other Spanish speakers. This codeswitching, however, is a completely different phenomenon from Mock Spanish.

29. I do make a claim to a sense of humor. But I have stopped using Mock Spanish, and I urge others to avoid it as well. As soon as Spanish is used within English in such a way that *de lujo* is as common as *de luxe*, that *camarones en mojo de ajo* are as prestigious a dish as *truite a la*

munière, and that *señorita,* like *mademoiselle,* can allude to good breeding as much as to erotic possibility, I'll go back to being as funny as possible with Spanish loan materials. Given the present context, I think that Mock Spanish is harmful—it is humor at the expense of people who don't need any more problems.

REFERENCES

Briggs, Joe Bob. 1987. *Joe Bib Briggs Goes to the Drive-in.* New York: Delacorte Press.

Cassidy, Frederick G. (ed.) 1985. *Dictionary of American Regional English. Volume I: Introduction and A-C.* Cambridge, MA: Belknap Press of Harvard University Press.

Chandler, Raymond. [1953] 1981. *The Long Goodbye.* New York: Vintage Books.

Essed, Philomena. 1991. *Understanding Everyday Racism.* Newbury Park, CA: Sage Publications.

Goldberg, David Theo. 1993. *Racist Culture.* Oxford: Blackwell's.

Gray, Hollis, Virginia Jones, Patricia Parker, Alex Smith and Klonda Lynn. 1949. Gringoisms in Arizona. *American Speech* 24:236.

Hill, Jane H. 1993a. Hasta la vista, baby: Anglo Spanish in the American Southwest. *Critique of Anthropology* 13:145–176.

Hill, Jane H. 1993b. Is it really "No problemo"? In Robin Queen and Rusty Barrett, eds., *SALSA I. Proceedings of the First Annual Symposium about Language and Society—Austin. Texas Linguistic Forum* 33:1112.

Hill, Jane H. 1995. The incorporative power of whiteness. Paper presented to the Annual Meeting of the American Ethnological Society, Santa Monica, CA, May 1995.

Louisor-White, Dominique, and Dolores Valencia Tanno. 1994. Code-switching in the public forum: New expressions of cultural identity and persuasion. Paper presented at the Conference on Hispanic Language and Social Identity, University of New Mexico, Albuquerque NM, February 10–12, 1994.

Morrison, Toni. 1992. *Playing in the Dark.* New York: Vintage Books.

Ochs, Elinor. 1990. Indexicality and socialization. In James W. Stigler, Richard A. Shweder, and Gilbert Herdt, eds., *Cultural Psychology,* pp. 287–308. Cambridge: Cambridge University Press.

Peñalosa, Fernando. 1980. *Chicano Sociolinguistics: An Introduction.* Rowley, MA: Newbury House Press.

Schulz, Muriel. 1975. The semantic derogation of women. In B. Thome and N. Henley (eds)., *Language and Sex: Difference and Dominance,* pp. 64–73. Rowley, MA:

Silverstein, Michael. 1979. Language structure and linguistic ideology. In Paul Clyne, William Hanks, aid Charles Hofbauer, eds. *The Elements: A Parasession on Linguistic Units and Levels,* pp. 193–247. Chicago: Chicago Linguistic Society.

Sperber, Dan and Deirdre Wilson. 1981. Irony and the use-mention on distinction. In Peter Cole, ed., *Radical Pragmatics,* pp. 295–318. New York: Academic Press.

Vélez-Ibáñez, Carlos. 1992. The emergence of the commodity identity of the Mexican population of the U.S. in cultural perspective. Paper presented to the 91st Annual Meeting of the American Anthropological Association, San Francisco, CA, December 2–5, 1992.

Van Dijk, Teun A. 1993. *Elite Discourse and Racism.* Newbury Park, CA: Sage Publications.

Williams, Raymond. 1977. *Marxism end Literature.* Oxford: Oxford University Press.

Woolard, Kathryn. 1989. Sentences in the language prison: The rhetorical structuring of an American language policy debate. *American Ethnologist* 16:268–278.

◈ WRITING/DISCUSSION EXERCISES

10.1   Read Jane Hill's "Mock Spanish" article. Write a short essay on how such examples of language use reflect underlying stereotypes and permit the continuation of racist attitudes toward others. Discuss your ideas with those of your classmates. Do all of you agree? Do some of you disagree? Discuss the areas of agreement and disagreement and see if you can analyze the source of any disagreement.

10.2   Professor Hill identifies three different "registers" of Anglo Spanish in the American Southwest. These can be referred to as "cowboy Spanish," "nouvelle Spanish," and "Mock Spanish." Briefly discuss each of these three registers. Give an example of each. How are they different from one another? How are they similar? Be prepared to discuss your examples with your classmates.

10.3   Pay attention to your own speech and to the speech of others around you. How many examples of Mock Spanish can you list in the space of one week? In what context was each example used? What do you think was the purpose of using the example? Do you think the speakers were aware of the hidden racism in these examples? Bring the results of your tally into class and compare it with the tallies of your classmates. Are the tallies similar? different? Compare the contexts and specifically the speech communities in which you and your classmates recorded your examples. How do they differ? How do the differences explain the different tallies?

10.4   Hill's article mentions the "Terminator" series of movies. What other movies can you think of in which there are examples of Mock Spanish? What about television shows? or greeting cards? Do you think the examples you found are meant to be funny? What makes them funny? Discuss these examples in class. See how large a list you and your classmates can compile. What does this list tell you about the culture in which these movies, television shows, and greeting cards are produced and consumed.

◈ WEB EXERCISES

10.1   Follow the links on the companion website about endangered languages. Write a short essay discussing some of the attempts that are being made to help people protect and revitalize their language. What are some of the issues and challenges that are involved? How are linguistic anthropologists helping?

10.2   Follow the links on the companion website about uncovering racism and sexism in language. Write a short essay summing up the challenges involved in recognizing how specific examples reveal underlying prejudices. Do the examples given seem clear to you? Why or why not? Discuss how language can convey racist and sexist ideas, even though the speakers of that language may be unaware of it and perhaps not intend it.

10.3   Follow the link on the companion website to the site of the Society for Linguistic Anthropology. Then follow the link to the most recent "web-enhanced" articles and read the
summaries of those articles. Write a short essay summing up the issues dealt with in those
articles. What are contemporary linguistic anthropologists writing about? In what ways
are these issues of interest or importance to you?

10.4   Search the InfoTrac database for articles about endangered languages and language
revitalization programs.

10.5   Search the InfoTrac database for articles about racism and sexism in language.

10.6   Search the InfoTrac database for articles about contemporary linguistic anthropology.

◈ GUIDED PROJECTS

Language Creating

If your instructor has assigned this project, this is the time to prepare a short skit to present to the rest of your class. Your skit should be entirely in your created language and you should be sure to use the proxemic and kinesic systems that your group invented for your language. A simple skit can be built around the idea of someone in your group asking someone else in your group to do something or to give something to someone. Your skit could open with a greeting and close with a farewell. The skit does not have to be long. Following the skit, if there is time, you should be prepared to describe and discuss the key features of the language that you have created. You should also prepare a notebook which sums up all the details of your group's language, to be handed in for grading. Your instructor will be your guide on which details to include and how to present them.

Conversation Partnering

If your instructor has assigned this project, this is the time to discuss the future with your conversation partner. Will you continue meeting or will you go your separate ways? For many students, conversation partnering marks the beginning of a long-term friendship with someone from another culture or country. For some, it is only a semester-long obligation. In either case, be sure to thank your conversation partner for his or her patience and help during the semester.

CREDITS

This page constitutes an extension of the copyright page. We have made every effort to trace the ownership of all copyrighted material and to secure permission from copyright holders. In the event of any question arising as to the use of any material, we will be pleased to make the necessary corrections in future printings. Thanks are due to the following authors, publishers, and agents for permission to use the material indicated.

Inside Cover: Courtesy of Hale Color Consultants, used by permission.

Chapter 1. 1–8: From "A Goy in the Ghetto: Gentile-Jewish Communication in Fieldwork Research," by William E. Mitchell, in *Between Two Worlds: Ethnographic Essays on American Jewry,* ed. Jack Kugelmass (Ithaca and London: Cornell University Press), pp. 225–239. Reprinted with permission of the author.

Chapter 2. 12–19: From "Hanunóo Color Categories," by Harold C. Conklin, *Southwestern Journal of Anthropology* 11(4): 339–344. Copyright © 1955 *The Journal of Anthropological Research.* Reprinted by permission. **23:** Courtesy of Rob MacLaury. Used by permission. **27:** Courtesy of Martin Ottenheimer. Used by permission.

Chapter 3. 30: Courtesy of Alan Joseph. Used by permission. **33:** The International Phonetic Alphabet, revised 1993, with 1996 updates. © International Phonetic Association, c/o Department of Linguistics, University of Victoria, Victoria, British Columbia, Canada. Used by permission. **34:** From K. L. Pike, *Phonemics: A Technique for Reducing Languages to Writing* (Ann Arbor: The University of Michigan Press). Copyright © 1947 University of Michigan Press. Reprinted by permission. **35:** From K. L. Pike, *Phonemics: A Technique for Reducing Languages to Writing* (Ann Arbor: The University of Michigan Press). Copyright © 1947 University of Michigan Press. Reprinted by permission. **41** (Chatino), **43** (KiSwahili), **44** (isiZulu, Totonac, Farsi): Excerpted and adapted from *Workbook in Descriptive Linguistics,* 1st ed., by Henry A. Gleason. © 1955. Reprinted with permission of Heinle, a division of Thomson Learning.

Chapter 4. 50: From *The Restaurant at the End of the Universe,* by Douglas Adams. Copyright © 1981 by Douglas Adams. Used by permission of Harmony Books, a division of Random House, Inc. **53** (Kanuri, LuGanda), **54** (Kurdish), **55–56** (Bontoc), **56** (Samoan), **57** (Tepehua): Excerpted and adapted from *Workbook in Descriptive Linguistics,* 1st ed., by Henry A. Gleason. © 1955. Reprinted with permission of Heinle, a division of Thomson Learning.

Chapter 5. 70–74: From "Native American Non-Interference," by Jimm Good Tracks, *Social Work* 18, no. 6. Copyright © 1973, National Association of Social Workers, Inc. Reprinted with permission.

Chapter 6. 79–82: From Joseph V. Hickey and William E. Thompson, "Personal Space: The Hidden Element of Cowboy Demeanor" (1988). Reprinted by permission of the authors.

Chapter 7. 88–97: From Harriet Ottenheimer, "Spelling Shinzwani: Dictionary Construction and Orthographic Choice in the Comoro Islands," *Written Language and Literacy* 4, no. 1 (2002): 15–29. © John Benjamins Publishing Company. Used by permission. **99:** Writing Systems: Japanese, adapted from *A Linguistics Workbook,* by Richard A. Demers